Add **Humor** to Your **Life**

Add **Life** to Your **Humor**

LINDSAY COLLIER

Published by Lindsay Collier, 2015

ISBN-13: 978-1519617972

ISBN-10: 1519617976

To Chris:
Thank you and enjoy.
My best to you

Some Comments About Lindsay's Books

I've had the benefit of Lindsay's advice for more years than we both want to admit. He developed the concept of "Humor in the Workplace" as a tool to be used with other creativity techniques to move your organization ahead of the pack. His advice is timeless; if you want to move beyond the "Guru of the Day" Lindsay is your man.

Lindsay Collier was the Art Buchwald of Eastman Kodak a couple decades ago. His musings were amazingly insightful then and just as relevant today. In this book, he simultaneously tickles your funny bone while making observations about how people deceive themselves and blunt their true potential every day. Read this book and you will see the world through different eyes. You will enjoy the trip.

Lindsay Collier is always at the top of the heap in terms of creativity. Sometimes I wonder if he levitates spontaneously. His concepts will keep you rolling off your chair and also thinking thoughts that will make you want to ice down your brain. Most authors write about "thinking outside the box." Heck, Lindsay always thinks outside the blimp. He is just in a different class from the other creative authors. Buy this book and enjoy a trip into the brain of a true genius.

Table of Contents

A Ten Day Program to Supercharge Your Humor

Books on Humor

Design of Humor Rooms

Comical Bumper Stickers

Add Humor to Your Life –Add Life to Your Humor

Introduction

We all have an absolutely wonderful resource available to us that can have a major influence on our lives. That resource is the ability to access our sense of humor – something we always have at our disposal. There are some 206 bones in the human body, and that's not counting the most important one - the **funny bone**. We all have one, but some of us can't seem to find it. Some people find it easy to use their sense of humor – and some don't. My purpose for writing this book is to help those of you who would like to bring humor more into your everyday lives. And, if humor is already a big part of your life, I'm hoping that some of the ideas in this book will enable you to raise the level even higher (think of it as tuning up your *funny bone*). Humor can make your life more exciting, more satisfying, more vibrant, and, perhaps even longer.

- o What part does humor play in your life?
- o Do you wake up with a smile on your face?
- o How often do you laugh and smile during the day?
- o Would you describe yourself as having a sense of humor?
- o Do others think you have a sense of humor?
- o Are you able to put a humorous spin on things that might appear at first to be serious?
- o If you work, do you think of "fun work" as an oxymoron?

It's been said that "laughter is like changing a diaper. It may not make a permanent difference but it sure improves things for a while". This is kind of funny – but it's also dead wrong! Laughter can definitely create a permanent change. And, in this book, I'm hoping to totally convince you of this, and give you the tools you can use to access your sense of humor and change your life.

I've been fascinated with humor as a resource for a long time. As a creative thinking and innovation expert in a major corporation, I facilitated hundreds of ideation sessions, and there is one thing I can say for sure. There was always a direct and positive relationship between the amount of laughter and the quality of the thinking derived from these sessions. At one point, I even built what may have been the first corporate **humor room** (more about this later) to help people bring more humor into the workplace.

In this book you will learn about the nature and characteristics of humor, why it is so important in your life, and what forms it takes. But, more importantly, you will walk away with dozens of great ideas on how to integrate humor into every aspect of your life. And, surprise, you may even have a few laughs in the process!

I am very excited about having the opportunity of sharing what I've learned about humor in my long career (longer than I would like to admit). I know you will enjoy this, and I'm hoping you are able to use the information here to add a lot of excitement and fun to your life.

This book will be in both paperback and Kindle form. It will also be available in other eBook formats. The Kindle and other eBook versions will have a distinct advantage since I will be referencing many internet sites for exploration. With the eBook versions you'll be able to directly link to these sites – something which is not possible with a paperback. In this paperback version, if you search the highlighted links using your favorite search engine, it should take you directly to the desired site. So why not purchase both versions? And while you are at it, make sure and buy an extra paperback copy for your guest bathroom. This will guarantee that you will have happy, smiling guests – and it will also get them out of your hair for a while as they sit in the bathroom for hours enjoying the book.

This book is laid out a bit differently than most. The five chapters deal with some great information about humor as well as some wonderful ways to use humor in your life. But in the Appendices, I plan to share some very powerful and useful material from my humor files, which I have been collecting for years. The appendix alone is worth the price for this book!

One more thing before we get started. I love to write, and am also an avid reader. It always bugs me when I read a book that contains a lot of what I would call *fluff*. Sometimes a little fluff is okay. But a lot of fluff that adds nothing but more pages to the book can be annoying. So I always apply an "anti-fluffinator" to my writing. My books may be shorter than *War and Peace* but nearly every word will add value. Enjoy!

Chapter 1

The Nature and Characteristics of Humor

"Sometimes your joy is the source of your smile, but sometimes your smile can be the source of your joy." — Thich Nhat Hanh

Let's start with the definition of humor which is quite simple. One dictionary defines humor as "the tendency of particular cognitive experiences to provoke laughter and provide amusement". Another defines it as "a quality that appeals to the sense of ludicrous and incongruous". Humor has no particular language – laughter and smiling are pretty much the same no matter where you come from. That has some important implications that we'll look at a little later. But humor also brings up an interesting "chicken vs. egg" question.

Am I happy because I'm laughing, or am I laughing because I'm happy? Which one comes first? Most people think they need something to make them laugh or smile to make them happy. In reality it works the other way as well. Laughing or smiling for no reason at all has the power to bring on the same happiness. I remember once seeing a bumper sticker that said, "Fake it till you make it". With humor, if you fake it there is a good chance that you will bring yourself into a humorous frame of mind. So you don't really have to wait for someone or something to tickle your funny bone. You can just begin laughing or smiling for no reason at all and get the same benefits as you would by listening to your favorite comedian. We will put this idea to use later.

More than 20 years ago I attended a conference on humor and one of the speakers was Dr. Annette Goodheart. She came out on the stage and said virtually nothing – rather strange for a speaker you might say. She began her presentation with a grin which turned into a smile and a quiet chuckle. This chuckle became an ever more intensive laugh, which ultimately became the most wonderful belly laugh I've ever heard. She never said a word, and yet the audience was in stitches. And they also brought home an important lesson – laughter, in and of itself, is enough to make you very happy. An interesting side note to this is that I clearly remember Dr.Goodheart's presentation after so many years, which says a lot about humor's impact on memory (more about that later too). While writing this, I *googled* Dr. Goodheart and was saddened to see that she passed away several years ago. We lost a great lady who had a very *good heart*.

The idea of laughter clubs or laughter yoga was introduced by Madan Kataria, M.D. in India in the mid-nineties. This form of therapeutic laughter combines element of group dynamics, principles of communication, sensory awareness, techniques of stress management and yoga in a form of positive physical expression.

This is sometimes referred to as *laughter yoga* which Wikipedia defines as:

> *A practice involving prolonged voluntary **laughter** based on the belief that voluntary laughter provides the same physiological, and psychological benefits as spontaneous laughter. Laughter yoga is done in groups, with eye contact and playfulness between participants. Forced laughter soon turns into real and contagious laughter.*

Have you ever noticed that it is difficult to engage in a hearty laugh when you are all by yourself? If you are alone and something really tickles your funny bone you will more likely have a good silent internal laugh, a chuckle, or a smile. This is probably not quite as beneficial as a nice loud belly laugh. So take the opportunity when possible to be with someone or, better yet, a group during those laughter periods.

One of the more prominent practitioners of humor here in the US is Steve Wilson, who calls himself "Cheerman of the Bored" at World Laughter Tour. He has trained several hundred *Laughter Leaders,* so you may want to check to see if there is a laughter club in your vicinity.

My experience is that men and women handle humor differently. Men tend to chuckle, and women tend to giggle. Although I have no real proof of this my feeling is that women are the winners when it comes to the ability to laugh and smile. However, babies are the real winners when it comes to laughter and smiling. It is said that a baby laughs 300 times per day, as opposed to us adults who laugh just 17 times per day (I wonder who did the counting). Adults between 18 and 34 laugh the most. And, only one out of the Seven Dwarfs laughs.

A YouTube of a baby laughing at paper ripping has chocked up more than 80 million views! Check it out **right now** – it'll get you off to a great start with this book! Since this is the one of the first hyperlinks in my book let me give you a quick explanation of how they work. If you have the paperback, just search the highlighted words with Google, Bing, Yahoo or whatever search engine you use, and it should come right up. If you are using the Kindle or eBook version, just click anywhere on the highlighted area and, voila, you are there. Click on "done" when , and you will be right back where you left off. Isn't technology great?

Humor is extremely contagious, and that is one reason why it is such an important factor in our lives. It is something you can easily spread, and easily catch. And your mission is to both spread it, and catch it. That's probably why people tend to laugh more when in groups. And it has no harmful effects. I don't know of anyone who has really "laughed themselves to death".

Humor is appropriate in almost any situation. Are there times when humor is not appropriate? Sure, there may be a few times when this is the case but they are few and far between. Some might tell you that humor is not appropriate during situations like sickness, loss, and grieving. The truth is that humor may be the most effective resource available in dealing with these situations. I have lost many of my loved ones and, in each case, my ability to apply humor to the situation played a major role in my recovery.

If you ever watched *Mash* on TV during its day, you observed many situations where humor was used in some serious medical situations. Its ability to help people in stressful situations is invaluable.

Humor can be used in positive and negative ways, and I have seen both. Positive humor brings people together, highly connects to the situation, comes from caring about others, and is often quite spontaneous. Negative humor tends to tear people apart, is often totally disconnected, can be quite contrived, and sometimes is used to mask incompetence, or cover up real feelings.

Try your best to always use humor in positive ways, and be aware of situations where humor is used in negative ways (by you or others). Humor used in negative ways can defeat all its advantages. My feeling is that, if you are a caring person, you don't have to worry about this at all.

Now let's take a look at the many ways that humor can have a positive impact on your life. Some of these might surprise and amaze you!

Chapter 2

Why is Humor So Important in Your Life?

Use your smile to change the world; don't let the world change your smile.

Anonymous

There are very few, if any, aspects of our lives that can't be positively affected by the use of humor. Learn how to access the tremendous power contained within your sense of humor, and you will begin to realize a plethora of benefits. There are many studies that try their best to support this, but I'm speaking mainly from my own experience – and I know how much it has meant to me.

As an expert in creative thinking, I have facilitated hundreds of ideation sessions in my corporate life. The effect of humor on creative thinking was quite obvious to me, so I began a rather intensive study which began with the reading *of The Anatomy of An Illness* by Norman Cousins (written in 1979). In this book he tells of how humor, he feels, actually saved him from a painful and, perhaps terminal, illness. This triggered much interest in the medical community, and there have been many studies since then into the effect of humor on the physical and mental well-being of us human beings.

I followed this up with some more extensive reading, study, application, and observation of humor in all aspects of life.

So let's take a look at how humor may affect our lives:

It can make you a healthier person by:

- o Strengthening your immune system
- o Reducing pain – triggering endorphins
- o Relaxing and toning muscles (including facial)
- o Reducing the effects of stress
- o Stimulating digestion and circulation (some think of as an internal organ massage)
- o Reducing blood pressure
- o Building up facial and throat muscles – reducing snoring
- o Cleansing the lungs – like deep breathing, sending more enriched oxygen to the body
- o Burning calories
- o Helping us live longer

o   Resting the brain
o   Keeping us from getting robbed

Okay, I admit, I threw in the last one just to see if you were paying attention. But I did read this somewhere and it makes sense. Maybe there is some truth that robbers will shy away from someone who is smiling. I hope you never get to experiment with this but, if you do, let me know if it works. If someone tries to rob you, flash them a big smile, and they make go on to the next person.

It can strengthen you mentally and emotionally by:

o   Helping to dissolve anger and unite people
o   Helping us deal with loss and grief
o   Helping us cope with change
o   Helping us remember things
o   Stabilizing mood swings
o   Increasing your attention span

It makes you a more interesting person by:

o   Attracting others with your smile
o   Helping to strengthen your relationships
o   Making you more attractive
o   Helping us communicate with people from other environments
o   Improving your morale
o   Enhancing romance
o   Stabilizing mood swings
o   Improving your outlook on life

It stimulates your thinking process by:

• Stimulating creative thinking
• Stimulating the problem solving process
• Helping the learning process
• Helping us get our message across

19

- Helping us remember

Wow! Think about it. You can gain all these advantages in your life just by accessing your ability to use the humor potential you carry around with you. I believe we all have that humor potential. Some of you may find it easy to access this potential, and some of you may not. My goal here is to maximize your opportunity to take full advantage of this humor potential.

You can be healthier, happier, smarter, friendlier, more attractive, emotionally strong, etc. etc. The list just goes on and on! Let's delve a little deeper into some of the specifics of how humor affects your life.

Norm Cousins, former editor of *The Saturday Review*, wrote a landmark book, *The Anatomy of an Illness*, which I believe paved the way for more study of the positive impact of laughter on the body. He had a very painful spinal disease in 1964 that kept him awake at night. He found that ten minutes of belly laughter would allow him to sleep pain free for 2 hours. He was given just a few months to live by his doctor, and told to get his house in order. His doctor told him he had a 1 in 500 chance of surviving the disease.

He fired his doctor, and left the hospital to check into a hotel. He ascertained that the cultural of defeat and over medication in the hospital was not going to be good for his health. He found a doctor who would work with him as a team member, as opposed to insisting on being in charge.

He obtained a movie projector (no small feat in those days) and a pile of funny movies, including the Marx Brothers and "Candid Camera" shows. He spent a great deal of time watching these films and laughing. And he didn't just laugh. In spite of being in a lot of constant pain, he made a point of laughing until his stomach hurt from it.

Can it be proved that laughing added 26 years to Norman Cousins' life? Not really. There can be no double blind tests for this. They can't take two groups of dying people and have one laugh and the other cry and see who lived. The ethical restraints would be enormous and there would be too many variables. We will just have to take his word. Perhaps this is a version of *Pascal's Wager*. If laughing doesn't extend life, wouldn't it be better to laugh anyway to make your last days more pleasant?

Norm Cousins was a humorous guy to begin with, as illustrated by this story about him:

He was admitted to the hospital for tests, and the nurse gave him the customary (back in the 60's) specimen bottle and a glass of apple juice. He decided to fill his specimen bottle with apple juice to see what happened. The nurse came back to see how he was doing, and picked up his specimen. She told him it looked very cloudy. He then took the specimen, drank it down, and said, "I'll just put this through the filters one more time."

So laughter can be a great way of reducing pain – and I would argue that this includes both physical and emotional pain. One way it reduces pain is just by providing a welcome distraction to it, and allowing us to just forget about our aches and pains. Laughter also reduces pain through the triggering of endorphins, which are chemicals in the brain that are natural pain killers. I like to think of these as tiny "Pac-men" that run around inside your body chewing up those nasty little *pain bugs*.

But wait – there's more! Laughter also strengthens the immune system by increasing natural killer cells and antibodies .And it relaxes muscles and tones facial muscles. Have you ever laughed so hard that your face actually hurt? Guess what – that's good for you. And some say it actually reduces snoring as well. There are also many studies that show that laughter reduces the effects of stress on the body. Laughter has also been suggested as a way of lowering blood pressure and exercising the heart.

Some suggest that laughter is akin to a good massaging of your internal organs. Some even refer to it as "internal jogging". Frequent belly laughter can empty your lungs of more air than it takes in, resulting in a cleansing effect, similar to deep breathing (and, I might add, a lot more fun).

That's just a little about the physical effects. How about the positive effects on your psyche? In my speaking tours in South Africa I came in touch with a native word that just fascinates me – ubuntu. Ubuntu, in its simplest form means, I am who I am through others. Your sense of humor is the best tool you have to create valuable relationships with those around you. Would you rather be with someone who has an outgoing sense of humor, or someone who is always dead serious? The tools and techniques in this book will help you to bring your relationships with your friends, family, associates, and, even strangers, to new levels.

Humor also has a tremendous positive effect on our thinking. We remember and retain things much longer that tickled our funny bone. Advertising folks know that. Funny ads will be remembered far longer than those dull ones. Think about some of the ads that had the greatest impact on you. I bet most of them involve humor.

Humor can often be the best way to solve conflicts. I believe it is pretty nearly impossible to be laughing with someone, and be mad at them at the same time. I remember several years ago reading about how the Troy, NY police used humor in some conflict situations. They were receiving a lot of calls regarding domestic arguments, and would sometimes answer the call with two officers, one dressed normally, and one dressed as Bugs Bunny. When someone answered the door, he would say, "What's up Doc?" Some of the conflicts ended right there. I'm going to take a wild guess that the one wearing the bunny costume was the rookie cop.

What about humor and grieving? I have experienced my share of loss in my life, the worst being the loss of my wife of 40 years, Jan, to ovarian cancer. With each loss, I have counted on my sense of humor to help me. And it has never let me down! The first sympathy card I received after losing Jan had the following:

In one of the stars I shall be living. In one of them I shall be laughing. And so it is as if the stars were laughing when you look at the sky at night.

From The Little Prince, Antoine de Saint-Exupery

The most helpful times I experienced during my bereavement have been those when we've been able to laugh at stories from the past. Humor is a great healer! After losing Jan, I wrote my book, <u>Surviving the Loss of Your Loved One; Jan's Rainbow</u>. And I have spoken to many bereavement groups about how to survive loss. Humor plays a very important part in my book, and my presentations.

How about humor in the workplace? Most of my career was with Eastman Kodak Company where I was an engineer, and also their expert in creative thinking and innovation (those were the good years). I know what you are thinking – isn't "humorous engineer" an oxymoron? I facilitated hundreds of ideation sessions in which I used many humorous techniques to get people thinking out of the box. At one point, I even built a *Humor and Creativity Room* to create an environment to stimulate laughter and creativity (see Appendix 8 for more information on this). This didn't go over too big with some management folks who probably last smiled when they had gas as a child. It was obvious to me that people who were laughing, smiling, and happy were much more physically, mentally, and creatively productive at work.

The words, "fun work" often tend to be an oxymoron like, "jumbo shrimp", "Senate ethics", and "professional wrestling". People often have a mindset that work is "5 days of pain for which you receive a 2- day reward". There are a few companies that recognize the value of humor at work, but this may be the exception rather than the rule. If your work experience contains no fun, then see what you can do to change that.

The effective use of humor can be very helpful in all business. It is so much more fun to deal with someone who has a nice smile and a fun-loving approach. I once saw a sign in a restaurant that said:

"We have an agreement with the bank. We don't cash checks and they don't serve pastrami sandwiches."

Isn't that much more pleasant than a "we don't cash checks here" sign?

Now let's take a look at the different forms humor can take.

Chapter 3

Various Forms of Humor

A person without a sense of humor is like a wagon without springs – jolted by every pebble on the road.

Henry Ward Beecher

Humor can take many forms, and I try to use as many of these as I can. The form of humor you use depends a lot upon the situation. I think that spontaneous humor, with a little touch of intention is the best. In other words, be as spontaneous as you can, but don't forget to think about who your audience is, and how this might affect them. You want your humor to lift others up, not put them down.

Somewhere in my days as a consultant I came across this list of formulas for humor. I never did know the source or I'd share it with you. It goes like this:

The Exaggeration Formula

"I'm so ugly that every night the kids flip a coin to see who gets to kiss me goodnight."

The Reversal Formula

"I have a job at the local radio station. Every morning I get into my car and report on the local helicopter traffic."

The Misdirection Formula

"Did you know that if you took a man's intestines out, and stretched them in a straight line, the man would die?"

The Cliché Rewrite Formula

"Old postman never die, they just lose their zip."

The Combination Formula

"The makers of Star Wars and Gandhi are making a new film, The Empire Turns the Other Cheek."

The Third Element Surprise Formula

"There are 3 ways to identify an antique. It must be 100 years old, be very rare, and be something nobody would want if there was another one."

The Joke Rewrite Formula

Modify a joke to make it relevant to the audience. I do this a lot.

The Malapropism Formula

"I guess I'll have to start from scraps."

The Difference Formula

"What's the difference between a tube and a crazy Dutchman? One is a hollow cylinder. The other is a silly Hollander."

The Definition Formula

"Gossip – mouth to mouth recitation."

The Pun Formula

"Add for a Korean PC – IBM with Seoul, gives you PC of mind."

Jokes

When you think of humor, most people immediately think of jokes. But jokes are just one form of humor – and may not always been the best choice. A lot of jokes tend to take victims. For example:

"What's the difference between a catfish and a lawyer? One is a bottom-feeding, scum-sucking predator. The other one is a fish".

Now, that's pretty funny – unless you're a lawyer. So you need to be sensitive when using this form of humor since your objective should be to use your humor in a positive and caring way. If you alienate someone with a joke, your application of humor will backfire on you.

I use to stay away from jokes (part of the reason is that I couldn't remember most of them), but I have learned through my experience that well-chosen jokes can be quite valuable. I often used *the joke rewrite formula* mentioned previously to make a joke friendlier and more suitable to the audience. I choose not to denigrate anyone with my jokes, but a lot of the so-called "Polish" jokes are actually quite funny. You just need to change them to fit the crowd you are with. For example, if you are with a bunch of old guys, make them "old guy jokes". I share some of my favorite jokes from my *Silly File* in Appendix 2.

In many cases shorter jokes work much better. Have you ever experience someone telling you a long joke when you felt like saying, "wake me up when you get to the punch line"? An example of a quick joke is:

> *An inebriated man and his drunken friend were sitting at a bar.*
> *"Do you know what time it is?", asked the drunk.*
> *"Sure," said the man*
> *"Thanks," said the drunk.*

There are a lot of sites on the internet where you can explore jokes. Here are a few to try:

The Laugh Factory Comedy Network

Aha Jokes

Funny and Jokes

There are dozens of joke sites on the internet. Just search for "jokes" and pick one (or 2, or 3, ---)

Quotes and Quips

As most of my followers know, I love quotations. One of my books (oh no, here comes another shameless book plug), *Quotations to Tickle Your Brain*, is a collection of some of my favorites. I use quotations a lot in my writing and my presentations, and I always try to have an interesting and funny quotation in my email signature.

Here are a few examples:

> If you see a fork in the road, take it. - Yogi Berra

> The similarities between me and my father are the same. - Dale Berra

From accident excuses:

> The guy was all over the road. I had to swerve a number of times before I hit him.

> I told them I was not injured but, when I removed my hat, I found I had a fractured skull.

> An invisible car came out of nowhere, hit me, and disappeared.

> The pedestrian had no idea which direction to go, so I ran over him.

From kids asked about what they learned in first aid class:

> For asphyxiation, apply artificial respiration until the victim is dead.

> For head colds, use an agonizer to spray the nose until it drops into the throat

Mother's excuse for school absence:

> Please excuse Tom for being absent. He had diarrhea and his boots leaked.

> Please excuse Ray Friday from school. He has very loose vowels.

Please excuse my son's tardiness. I forgot to wake him up and did not find him untill I started making the beds.

Maryann was absent December 11-16, because she had a fever, sore throat, headache, and upset stomach. Her sister was also sick, fever and sore throat, and her brother had a low grade fever and ached all over. I wasn't the best either, sore throat and fever. There must have been a flu going around. Her father even got hot last night.

My son is under a doctor's care and should not take Physical Education today. Please execute him.

From Murphy's Laws of Combat Operations:

If your attack is going really well then it's an ambush.

Pleasant Incongruities

Often you can turn humorous incongruities into a great source of laughter. I remember once when I was waiting in my doctor's office and picked up a brochure called "You and Dandruff". Right now that doesn't sound that funny. But it sure tickled my *funny bone* at the time. Can you remember some of these instances in your life?

Can an add about a funeral home make you laugh? I saw an ad for a funeral home in Buffalo, New York, and the name of it was Amigone. Could there really be a funeral home called *Am I Gone*? If you don't believe me, check it out at Amigone.com.

For some reason, church bulletins often contain humorous incongruities:

Sermon tonight – What is Hell? Come early and see the choir practice.

There will be a bean and taco dinner tonight at the church. A program of special music will follow.

There will be a meeting of the Little Mother's Club tonight. All those wishing to become Little Mothers, please meet the minister in his study at 7 pm.

Sometimes incongruities appear in business advertisements:

Bakery. Get your buns in here.

Beauty Salon. Ears pierced while you wait.

Restaurant ~ Special Today, T-Bone 60 cents, with meat, $9.95.

Veterinarian – John Jones, Veterinarian and Taxidermist. Either way you get your dog back.

In a Podiatrist's office - Time wounds all heels.

On a Septic Tank Truck - Yesterday's Meals on Wheels.

At a Proctologist's door - To expedite your visit, please back in.

On a Plumber's truck - We repair what your

husband fixed.

On another Plumber's truck - Don't sleep with a drip. Call your plumber.

On a church's billboard - 7 days without God makes one weak.

On a Maternity Room door - Push! Push! Push!

Outside a muffler shop - No appointment necessary. We hear you coming.

In a Veterinarian's waiting room - Be back in 5 minutes. Sit! Stay!

And don't forget the sign at a radiator shop - Best place in town to take a leak.

Cartoons and Comics

They say a picture is worth a thousand words, which makes this source of humor particularly beneficial. Some of my favorites are

- Far Side
- Quigmans
- Rubes
- Dilbert
- Sydney Harris

Everyone should start their day reading a few newspaper comic strips. And a great place to check out some great comics is a card store. You may also want to check out GoComics.com , a site for some of the best comic strips.

Humor as Akido

I tried to come up with a definition of Aikido but, the more I looked into it, the more confused I became. And then I figured that, if I tried to pass this on to you, then we'd both just leave confused. So here is my simple explanation.

If someone attacks you (physically or verbally) you have you have four options:

- Run

- Fight Back
- Get Nailed
- Roll With it

Aikido is a Japanese form of Jujitsu that deals with the last option – rolling with it. I believe there is an interesting form of humor that tends to just, "go with the flow". Maybe a good example will make his a bit clearer. This one came from Joel Goodman at one of his humor conferences.

> You receive an obscene phone call and the caller says, "I would like to take your panties off". Your Aikido response would be, "I didn't know you were wearing my panties".

One day I was at my doctor's complaining of severe pain in my knee. He suspected it was gout but, to find out, he needed to extract some fluid from behind my kneecap. He pulled out a large hypodermic needle and began preparing it. When he saw the look of fear on my face he said, "I saw this done on TV once". What a difference that made – a perfect Aikido!

Aikido humor may be a little more difficult to master because it tends to demand a spontaneous reply. Look for some opportunities to use some "go with the flow" humorous responses. It's a good way to make friends.

Spaced Out Stuff

I first discovered this, and decided to include this in my list of humor forms after reading a book called, The Book of Stupid Questions, by Tom Weller. This book contains questions such as:

- Would you rather think you were smart but really be dumb, or really be smart and think you are dumb?
- Would you rather be roasted alive over mesquite charcoal or force fed tofu until you burst?

- If you found that you had been mixed up in the hospital as a baby, would you turn yourself in?
- What kind of hen lays extra-large eggs?
- Why do ants congregate on sidewalks?
- Why do exterminators wear hard hats?
- When a fly alights on a ceiling, does it do a loop, or a roll to get into position?

And then I got into reading some of David Feldman's *Imponderables* books such as:

- Why Do Clocks Run Clockwise?
- How Does Aspirin Find a Headache?
- Are Lobsters Ambidextrous?
- When Do Fish Sleep?

One of my favorite comedians, Steven Wright, uses spaced-out humor almost exclusively. See Appendix 4 for more about him and all my other favorite funny people. Here are a few of his comments:

I bought a humidifier the other day and then decided to buy a de-humidifier, put them in the same room, and watch them fight it out.

If you are traveling at the speed of light in your car and turn the headlights on, does anything happen?

I pleaded insanity for a parking ticket.

Whenever I go to have my teeth cleaned, I always eat a whole box of Oreo cookies just before my appointment.

I named my last dog *Stay*. Drove him crazy. Here, Stay. Hear, Stay!

Dave Barry, one of the funniest authors ever, also uses a lot of this type of humor. More about Dave Barry later.

So this type of humor is really just "think out of the box" humor. It takes a little practice sometimes but it's a blast to use! It also has a nice side benefit, in that it tends to stimulate your creativity.

The key thing is to use a form of humor that you are comfortable with. But it's a good idea to mix it up some too. You don't want people to get bored with the sameness of your humor. And, remember, always use it in positive, caring ways.

Now let's move on to what is, perhaps, the most important part of this book. In the next chapter, we'll take a journey through some ways you can add more humor to your life. I know you will enjoy this journey.

Chapter 4

How Can You Use Humor
in Your Life?

Humor is mankind's greatest blessing.

Mark Twain

In my book, **How to Live Happily Ever After; 12 Things You Can Do to Live Forever**, I begin by mentioning Earle Nightingale's Secret of Life. That secret is, *You Are What You Think,* and I believe we all need to recognize how important a statement that is. If you think of yourself as a fun-loving person there is a good chance you will be one, or become one. If you think you are a dud, you may become a dud.

So how can you make humor a powerful influence in your life? Begin by taking yourself and everything that is happening around you lightly. Of course, there will be some exceptions when you will have no choice other than to be deadly serious. But I believe these are few and far between. As the saying goes, "Don't take life too seriously, you'll never get out of it alive". I try my best to put a humorous spin on just about everything. But, you do need to be sensitive and caring in how you use humor so you don't give people the impression that you are making fun of a situation which they may think is too serious for humor.

Following are my suggestions for how to best add humor to your life, and add life to your humor. Some of them are pretty obvious and some are just downright crazy. I guarantee that, if you make these suggestions a part of your everyday life, you will be happier, healthier, more fulfilled, and have much healthier relationships with the people around you. So here goes!

Be a "Gluten for Funishment".

What on earth is a "gluten for funishment"? It is someone who just sees the humor in everything around him or her. When you take everything around you lightly, it's easy to find something humorous about nearly everything you see or hear. And, if something doesn't pop up right away, then just look a little deeper. As I am writing this I am looking out the window of our Upstate New York summer place which is in a very nice spot on the edge of the woods. I'm watching two chipmunks chase each other around the yard, and being thoroughly entertained. My day may be brighter because of these two *cuties*. And, as I am watching this, my thoughts go to many years ago when my sister and brother and I would chase each other around our yard. Many of the ideas and techniques in this book are designed to make you a better "gluten". But it starts with your ability to see humor in just about everything.

Here's an example I recall from my own experience. One day I was driving to a meeting at a satellite plant along a highway that had just been striped. I was looking at the new yellow stripe along the shoulder and there was a dead raccoon in its line that had just been painted right over with the stripe. Maybe that's not that funny (certainly not for the raccoon), but I couldn't stop laughing to myself. I think I even used this story to illustrate a point during our meeting.

If you are not one of those folks who just naturally sees humor in most everything, you'll have to work at it. Make it a point to become a better observer, and also make it a point to find (or make up) something humorous about what you see. I guarantee you'll enjoy the experience, and it will really help you add some zest to your humor.

Use Happy Words – Avoid Unhappy Ones.

The words we use go a long way towards making us who we are. What kind of words do you tend to use in your conversation, and in your thought process? Are they happy, positive, exciting, fun-loving, daring, uplifting words? Here are a few to get you started. For a more complete list of happy words see Appendix 3.

Agreeable	Effervescent
Alive	Elated
Beautiful	Enjoyable
Blessed	Excellent
Blissful	Exceptional
Brilliant	Excited
Bubbly	Exuberant
Caringly	Fabulous
Celebratory	Fortunate
Cheerful	Friendly
Contented	Fun-loving
Contentment	Giggly
Creative	Glad
Delighted	Good-humored
Delightful	Great
Distinguished	Happiness
Ecstatic	Happy

Heavenly	Kind
Helpful	Liking
Honored	Lively
Hopeful	Lovely
Inspired	Magnificent
Jovial	Romantic
Joyful	Satisfied
Jubilant	Spectacular
Just	Wonderful

You want to use more happy words in your thoughts and conversations. But you also want to try to avoid sad/unhappy words. Here are a few words to avoid:

Bleak	Morose
Dark	Oppressed
Depressed	Sad
Despair	Scared
Dismal	Somber
Downcast	Sorrow
Gloomy	Sullen
Hopeless	Tears
Jaded	Unhappy
Misery	Upset

If you find yourself in the "happy word" side of the fence, congratulations! You'll find the use of humor in your life to be much easier. If you tend toward the "unhappy" word side, you need to make an effort to change. It may not be easy, and may involve a bit of work on your part. Start by trying your best to think in terms of happy words, followed by a concerted effort to use these in your conversations with others. At the same time, try your best to avoid the unhappy words.

Smile and Laugh a Lot.

Smiling is just a mild form of laughter, but it's a great beginning. As they say," smiling changes your face value". Begin each day with a smile, even if you have to force yourself into it. Get up, look yourself in the mirror, and flash the biggest, silliest, stupidest grin you can come up with. Then raise this smile to a new, higher level till the corners of your mouth nearly meet your ear lobes. You might want to make sure nobody is watching you, or they might take steps to have you committed. If you feel down during the day for some reason, then repeat this process if you can.

Try to carry your smile with you all day. That doesn't mean you need to be constantly smiling, but it does mean you need to be ready to smile at all times. Incidentally, if you have difficulty perfecting your smile you may want begin by using a *smile stick*. You can order these at smilestick.com for just a few bucks. Keep some in your home, office, car, or wherever you think might be appropriate.

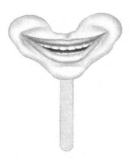

For years while I was driving back and forth to work, I would carry one in my car, and I found a number of opportunities to put it to good use. For example, if I pulled up to one of those people who looked like death-warmed-over on their way to work, I would flash them a big grin with my smile stick. I think in some cases it made their day – and it also helped me to start mine on a positive, happy note.

Smile at everyone you encounter. Never miss the opportunity to smile at someone you meet, or just pass by. You don't always need the ear to ear smile – just a pleasant smile that says you are glad to see them may suffice. A nice greeting along with it is always welcome too. You'll feel good and they probably will too.

Always look for an opportunity to share some laughter with the people you meet. If something tickles your funny bone don't hesitate in sharing this with those around you, even if they are total strangers. And never bypass an opportunity to laugh (with gusto if possible) when someone shares something with you that they think is funny. If it isn't that funny then just fake it a bit.

Find your "Smile Mindset".

We all have had certain instances in our lives when something struck us so funny that we nearly *laughed until we cried*. The idea here is to save these, and file them away so that you can bring them up whenever you feel the need. Let me give you an example of this.

My oldest son attended college about an hour away from our home. He was home visiting us one weekend, and he and I were watching a rather silly game show on TV. The announcer made the statement that the first place winner would get a nice cash prize, and the runner-up would get a year's supply of *Riceroni*. I thought that was somewhat funny, but my son was in stitches, and just couldn't stop laughing. He would stop for a while, and then break out in another fit of laughter. This turned out to be one of his "smile mindsets" and, to this day (this was somewhere around 25 years ago), if he is feeling down, all I need to say is *Riceroni* , and it'll brighten his day.

Your smile mindset might be just something you once heard that struck you so funny that it occupies a permanent spot in your brain. Omni magazine once ran a Creative Science Theories Contest. The winner and follow-up were:

"When a cat is dropped, it always lands on its feet. And when toast is dropped, it always lands with the buttered   side facing down. I propose to strap buttered toast to the back of a cat; the two will hover, spinning inches above the ground. With a giant buttered cat array, a high-speed monorail could easily link New York with Chicago".

" If an infinite number of rednecks, riding in an infinite number of pickup trucks, fire an infinite number of shotgun rounds, at an infinite number of highway signs, they will eventually produce all the world's great literary works in Braille".

This was probably about 25 years ago too, and I still vividly recall them. And, if I ever need a little help nudging my humor, I can just visualize that cat hovering above ground.

So. think of 3-4 things from your past where you had this experience. File them away, and assign each one of them some sort of trigger that will bring them quickly back to your mind. A trigger might be squeezing one of your fingers, scratching your nose, pulling your ear, or similar activity. Whenever you are feeling down, or just feel the need to lighten up, bring one of these up and have a good laugh about it.

Another good use of the smile mindset is to keep track of some of the humorous instances experienced by your friends and family. Then, if one of them is a bit down, or experiencing some sadness, you can lift them up by reminding them of this instance. This is a great way to nurture caring relationships.

Keep a Silly File (or two).

Life is full of funny moments, and the idea here is to capture and save as many of these as you can. Hardly a day goes by without several things occurring to me that tickled my funny bone. And I hate to lose these, so I try to capture as many as I can. Since most of these come to me via my email, or cruising a number of blogs and websites, I find it very useful to put them in what I call my "Silly File" on my computer. If you are a computer savvy person, my suggestion to you is to establish a Word file, and copy and paste anything that strikes you funny to that file. At this point my personal "Silly File" is huge. Every now and then I need to go and clean it up and, needless to say, this is an enjoyable task.

I also keep a hard copy folder which I file right in front of my "bills to be paid" file. I put it there so I'll have something to laugh about when paying bills. So my suggestion to you is to keep both a paper, and a digital "Silly File".

Visit these files often, particularly if you are feeling a little down. Prior to giving one of my presentations, I always take a little trip through these files to pick out some humor that will be appropriate for my audience. I'm a firm believer that the best form of humor is that which connects directly with your audience.

I have included a pretty good example of snippets from my file in Appendix 2 for your entertainment and use. This would be a good start for the development of your own file. Feel free to copy and paste and use these to your heart's content. And, if you would like me to send you a digital copy, just email me at lindsaycollier@comcast.net. This would be a good way to get your file started.

Do Silly Stuff.

One of my first books was called, *Get out of Your Thinking Box: 365 Things You Can Do to Brighten Your Life and Stimulate Your Creativity*. I wrote this as a compilation of things to do to help people think differently, and more creatively. I've facilitated hundreds of ideation sessions in my time as an expert in creative thinking, and know from experience that giving people the opportunity to take breaks on the "silly side" can really change their thinking.

When I first began my consulting business, I remember one day reading in our local business paper about some people who had been promoted. I felt left out because it was just me, and who could I promote? My Golden Retriever, Molly, was sitting by my side as usual, and I thought, why not promote her? So I sent a press release promoting Molly, and the next week among the promotions was listed. *"Molly Collier has been promoted to Chief Operation Officer of Creative Edge Associates"*. I took her for an extra-long walk and gave her a big bone that evening to celebrate her promotion. It was a very good day! I thought I would do it again, and include a picture. I wish I had!

Here are a few examples of some silly stuff you may want to do. There are more in Appendix 5. But don't just stick with my examples – try to invent some of your own!

- Call a random number and just wish someone a nice day.
- Look at the world as if your eyes were on your knee caps.
- Come up with a nonsense language and use it with your friends.
- Go to a bank and ask for change for a nickel.
- Think of all the ways your life is like a *slinky*.
- Go test drive an 18 wheeler.
- Spell check all your friends names and see what comes up. One of my friends' names came up as "cheery hormones".
- Pretend you are a sponge for a day, and soak up everything you can. Wring yourself out at the end of the day. If your name is 'Bob" skip this one.
- Write down all the things that are bothering you on a roll of toilet paper – and flush it.

- Read a Dr. Seuss book.
- Pick a few objects around you and try to see what it would be like to be those objects.

Take Lots of Humor Breaks.

Whenever you begin to feel that you're getting just too darn serious about things, take a humor break. It can be a quick break (stand up, take a deep breath, and smile) or a more substantial one. This book is loaded with ways you can do this, so take your pick. Visit a comical website, read a humorous cartoon book, visit your "Silly File", watch a funny video, go to a toy store, etc. The important thing is to get away from your seriousness for a while, and put yourself back into a humorous frame of mind.

This may be especially important if you are experiencing some stress. Humor may be the best anecdote ever for stress. If you can pinpoint the source of your stress, then you can try to apply some form of humor to that source. For example, if your stress is coming from dealing with your children, you might want to conjure up a few comical metaphors about dealing with children. For example, dealing with kids is like nailing Jell-O to the wall, herding cats, selling tofu at the county fair, etc. The more you can think in terms of these comical metaphors, the more your chances are of taking a lighter look at the problem, and relieving your stress. Try this out the next time your stress button is pushed.

Here are a few things you may want to do in your humor break:

o Cruise the net for humorous stuff. Just think of a humorous word and get started.
o Watch Funny Movies or shows.
o Peruse your "Silly File".

- o Check out the baby laughing link mentioned earlier. While at it, check out more baby laughing videos. See if you can laugh like them! Or, better still, find a baby and make them laugh.
- o Observe some infants at play.
- o Think of some of the funniest moments in your life.
- o Check out your favorite comedian's site on YouTube (see Appendix 4).
- o Walk around using your "smile stick" to smile at people.
- o Read the "funny papers"'.
- o Send some jokes or funny quips to friends.

Do Some Humaerobics.

Every now and then, you just need to take a real aggressive humor break and do something that really charges up your funny bone. Think of this as a kind of *"humor defibrillator"*. The next chapter will give you some good examples of these. When the opportunity exists, try these in group situations. They can do wonders in stimulating a group's energy.

Use Metaphors and Other Creative Exercises.

Metaphors are one of best ways I know to help people think creatively. Part of the reason for this is that most metaphors have the ability to conjure up some pretty good humor. They also allow us to apply some very different rules to our thinking.

Here are a few metaphors I have used to stimulate humor and creative thinking in my days as a creative process consultant. Use these to answer the question, "Why is my situation like a ----?" Feel free to add your own to the list.

- A Mud Slide
- Jell-O with Fruit
- Silly Putty
- The Titanic
- A Dinosaur
- A Flower Garden
- An Elephant
- A Game of Scrabble
- Spaghetti & Meatballs
- An Ice Cream Sunday
- A Flea Market
- An Old Dog
- Jack in the Box
- A Slinky
- A Rubber Chicken
- A Cage of Birds
- A Compost Pile
- Various Internal Body Organs
- A Stir Fry
- The Senate and the House
- A Shopping Mall
- A Spider Web
- Buffalo Chips
- Earth Worms
- Tooth Plaque
- A Can of Sardines
- Panty Hose

A technique I have used extensively which I call "*mental bungee jumping*" involves taking your thinking to entirely new boundaries. The object here is to stretch your thinking to an absolute extreme, and then bounce back to make this a reality. This can be a real blast! It can also result in some very funny outcomes.

As I've said before, creativity and humor are closely entwined. Anything that gets you thinking more creatively almost always tickles your funny bone. Likewise, anything that makes you laugh or smile almost always stimulates your creativity.

I could go on and on about various creative thinking techniques, but it might fill up this book. In my book (oh no, not another shameless book plug), **Organizational Mental Floss; How to Squeeze Your Organization's Thinking Juices,** I get into more extensive discussions of the use of metaphors and other techniques.

Work on Being a Total Optimist.

"A pessimist sees a sand trap next to every green, an optimist sees a green next to the every sand trap". Which one are you? Although I have no proof of this, I believe that optimists have a much better chance of having a good sense of humor than pessimists. I've spent a lot of time observing and thinking about people's behavior, and have noticed that those who have a positive, optimistic outlook on life tend to be the most humorous. Those who tend towards thinking in negative terms have difficulty letting their humor potential out.

While writing this, I received a short video from a friend that I'd love to share with you. It is one of the sweetest statements of optimism I've ever seen. It's called :

A Magical Moment with My Grandfather

and may turn you immediately into an eternal optimist. Check it out.

In my book, **How To Live Happily Ever After; 12 Things You Can Do to Live Forever**, I have a whole chapter on being an optimist – I think it's that important. Here is a wonderful short story from the book to keep in mind.

> *It was Christmas and a little boy and girl were very excited to see what Santa had left, so they snuck down a little early to take a peak. The only thing they saw was a large pile of manure next to the tree. The little boy ran back to his room crying, thinking that he must have behaved very badly to deserve this. The little girl ran to the woodshed to get a shovel, came back and began shoveling like mad saying, "There must be a pony in here somewhere."*

For another great message about optimism check out "The Black Dot; A Beautiful and Inspiring Story" on the net.

If you feel you are a true optimist, congratulations! You should have no problem using humor. If you are drifting more to the pessimist end, then work on becoming more of an optimist. It'll help you access your humor potential and make you a happier person overall.

There is also another option - being a realist. Sailors use the following example of realists:

The pessimist complains about the wind.

The optimist expects it to change.

The realist adjusts the sails.

Another example of being a realist would be someone who makes this statement:

"While you all were arguing about whether the glass was half full, or half empty, I drank it".

I'm thinking that being an optimistic realist is the best option.

Be Someone's Reason to Smile.

They say that, when you help others, you always help yourself as well. Remember, humor is very contagious too. If you make it a point to use your own sense of humor while with your friends, family, and associates, you will be giving them all more incentive to do the same.

It doesn't have to been a huge effort. Just smiling at someone can often make their day. And, following that up with a statement telling them they have a nice smile can really make their day. I always try to make it a point to have my friends be happier after being with me than they were before. And you should too. Have you made someone smile today?

Overcome the "Fun Work is an Oxymoron" Syndrome.

I don't know about you, but I just can't imagine life without humor. But the fact is that the majority of people spend a good portion of their lives working in organizations where "fun work" is an oxymoron. I have facilitated hundreds of ideation, or brainstorming, sessions and can unequivocally say that the use of humor in these sessions pretty much always guaranteed success. Where there is laughter there is creativity. And my most requested presentation from corporations and organizations was always, *Humor in the Workplace*.

But, that's just the beginning. Remember, humor has the power to reduce stress, improve health, build strong relationships, improve communications between people, strengthen the learning process, and help people cope with change. And how important are all these elements in creating highly effective work systems?

So many people think of work as "five days of pain for which you receive a two day reward". I have always made it a point to be an observer of people's behavior. And each day, as I drove to work, I'd make it a point to see how happy, or unhappy, people looked. The *unhappies* always outnumbered the *happies*. There were always a few cars with bumpers sticker saying something like, "A bad day fishing beats a good day at work". It was rare to see anyone smiling so I would try to flash them a smile. While sitting at a streetlight I would sometimes even flash my "Smile Stick" at them. You should always carry one of these in your car.

The majority of work areas are designed to be either very functional, or to look good. Creative thinking does not tend to flourish in the typical sterile environment that fits these characteristics. Often people just need a place to escape to that allows them to just get outside of their normal thinking box. I was the main driver behind the development of the **Kodak Humor and Creativity Room** in 1991. This was arguably the first corporate humor room ever built and, for the most part, management wasn't too happy about it. After all, most of them last laughed when they had gas as a child! See Appendix 9 for more information about the design of a humor room.

Start all Events, Meetings, and Gatherings off With Humor.

In my many years as an expert in creativity and innovation in the workplace, I have facilitated hundreds of meetings. Many of these meetings were designed to bring out creative thinking and new ideas. I don't believe I ever started a meeting on a serious note. I always tried to come up with something (a joke, a quote, a funny story, a crazy exercise, etc.) to begin the meeting with laughter.

I don't run these meetings anymore, but have continued to carry on this same idea whenever I get a chance. This might be having friends over, walking into a roomful of people, meeting friends for golf, beginning a presentation, or just every day meetings with people. Never pass up an opportunity to start an activity by brightening everyone's day. You'll make these activities more enjoyable for everyone – including yourself. And enjoyable translates to effective!

If you are still involved in organizational life and want to begin meetings with laughter, my book (here comes another one of those shameless plugs), Organizational Mental Floss, How to Squeeze Your Organization's Thinking Juices, contains a whole chapter of techniques you can use.

Start EVERY DAY With a Cup of Laughter.

Some people wake up happy, and some don't. Which one are you? For the most part, I wake up happy every day. But on those occasions where I don't, I try to do something to bring my *funny bone* back to life. Sometimes it's just a matter of looking into the

55

mirror and flashing myself a big smile. Sometimes it may be necessary to try out some of those things in my section on humaerobics breaks.

Either way, it is just important to start your day with some humor, and that should stay with you all day.

Exaggerate.

Exaggeration is a fun form of humor. The key to using exaggeration is to inflate or deflate whatever you are talking about so much that it is obviously an exaggeration. It's a bit of a balancing game, balancing truth with exaggeration. I heard someone say once, "Some folks never exaggerate - they just think big". So, if you have trouble exaggerating - just try to think big (or sometimes small).

Practice the art of exaggeration by picking a certain subject and brainstorming humorous ways to make it much bigger or smaller. For example, if you just got a birdie playing golf complete this sentence:

The last time I had a birdie was.

> Just after the War of 1812.

> When Eisenhower was President.

> The same day I got my first chest hair.

Have fun with this and you will soon be an expert in spontaneous exaggeration, and able to wow all your friends, as well as entertain them. If you fish, you know how to exaggerate because nothing makes a fish bigger than almost being caught.

Add Humorous Quotes to All Your Messages.

I've always had somewhat of a love affair with quotations. I've used them extensively in my presentations and training. In one of my books (here comes another shameless plug), <u>Quotations to Tickle Your brain</u>, I share some of my favorites which I collected during my years as a creative thinking process expert. A correctly chosen quote is a great way to get a point across, and to get people thinking creatively. And the use of humorous quotes is a great way to lighten up any situation. In Appendix 1 you will find some very interesting quotes to get you started.

Look for humorous quotations, and start your own list of favorites. Then spread them around in your email or text messages, and use them at appropriate times in your conversations. I always have one in my email signature, and change it often. Find some creative ways to share these with your friends and family. Pick a few of your favorites and commit them to memory. Then wait for opportunities to fit them into conversations.

For example, in a recent conversation the topic was about right hand vs. left. This gave me the opportunity to use one of my favorite quotations:

"I'd give my right arm to be ambidextrous."

Although this is not a Yogi Berra quote, his hilarious quotes may be a good starting point or you. You can find these easily by searching, "Yogi Berra Quotes", on Google or any other search engine.

Here are a few ways you might use your humorous quotations:

- o Add one to your email signature and change often.
- o Put one on your business or personal card.

- Pick one each day to guide you through the daily bumps.
- Stick one on your car's visor - change it often.
- Print them on stickers and place on your mail.
- Send them to your internet friends.
- Post your favorites on Facebook or Pinterest.
- At meetings, give each person a quote to share.
- Use as a screensaver of your computer.
- Give them to strangers who really look unhappy.
- Tape one under random chairs at a meeting and have people share.

Hang Around Humorous People – Avoid, or Change, Others.

Your ability to make humor a powerful part of your life is made easier if you spend more time with those you know have a great sense of humor. As I've said before, it is highly contagious. But it may be quite rare to have all your friends, family, and associates be naturally humorous.

The next best thing is to do all you can to help them become more humorous. Try to use your own sense of humor in a way that allows them to lighten up. There are a lot of ideas and techniques in this book that you can use to help your all-too-serious friends loosen up. Make it a point to let your humor spill off onto all your friends. Who is a person in your life who you would like to be closer to, but who is also rather un-humorous? Start with that person and see if you can make her or him a more humorous person. It'll really make you feel good.

Let Go of Things That Sadden You.

Avoid conversations, news, entertainment, etc. that frighten, sadden, distress, or upset you. It's hard to tickle your funny bone when you are in a sad state of mind. Unfortunately, our lives aren't always jam-packed with upbeat news and happenings.

So the next best thing is to be able to apply your sense of humor to turn these issues into a more positive, humorous framework.

One of my mentors, Sidney Shore, shared a technique with me years ago which he called, "What's good about it?". This involved thinking about all the things that were" good" about a particularly bad problem, or situation. The idea was then to see how some of these "good things" could be used to solve the problem. I have tried to make this a part of my life for years - and it works!

Always Smile While on the Phone.

Try this out sometime. Record yourself reading a short paragraph while frowning, and forcing yourself to feel sad. Then do it again while smiling. Did you see a difference? I bet you did. When you are smiling, people on the phone with you will know that, and the conversation will likely be much more rewarding. Warning! Do not smile when receiving an obscene phone call.

Join, or Start a Laughter Club.

Laughter Clubs (sometimes referred to as laughter yoga) are cropping up all over the place. They are loosely defined as informal groups of people who get together to laugh as a form of exercise.

They are mostly fully independent, not-for-profit, non-political, non-religious, and non-community-based associations of people who just choose to be happy. No one needs permission to start a laughter club. They do not report to anybody, are not told what to do, and do not pay royalties to anybody.

I live in Florida, in a place called the Villages. We have a wonderful monthly meeting of laughter yoga run by a charming couple. Even I was a little leery at first, but it took about a minute and a half to really get into it. And, I always leave with a big smile on my face.

If you are looking for a laughter club near you, try visiting Social Laughter Clubs. If you can't find one, and think you have the ability, consider starting one yourself, or with some friends.

Chapter 5

Humaerobics and Humor Exercises

People do not quit playing because they get old.
They get old because they quite playing.

If you don't exercise your body regularly, it can get soft and weak. If you don't exercise your mind regularly, you'll lose mental sharpness. And, if you don't exercise your sense of humor on a regular basis, you may not be able to reach your potential here as well.

If you fully engage in the 20 suggestions in the last chapter, you should have no problem maintaining, and building up your funny bone. Think of this chapter as extra credit. Here we will take a look at a few things you can do to really let your sense of humor blossom. And many of the exercises here are done in groups, so they have the capability of letting a lot of humor out of the bag.

As I've said before, I spent many years as an expert in creative thinking and innovation in organizations, and worked with many groups, helping to get them to take their thinking to places it's never been. Some of the exercises here are meant to be done on an individual basis, and some are meant to be applied in group situations. Use your own creativity to work them any way you want. And don't be afraid to let your laughter loose.

Stand, Breath, and Smile

Let's start with an easy one that you can do anytime. I suggest you do this when you get up each morning, preferably in front of a mirror. Just stand real tall, take a deep breath, and flash the biggest, perhaps silliest looking smile you can. If you are with someone, or with a group of people, show your smile to everyone you can. And, every time you pass a mirror, flash yourself a big smile. You may even want to keep your *smile stick* handy just in case you don't really care to smile at that moment.

Silly Walks

I was hooked on Monty Python's Flying Circus back in the 70's and still love to watch re-runs. One skit that has stuck with me over the years is *The Ministry of Silly Walks*, Check this out -right now!

As a creative process consultant, I have used this many times in groups to help them really loosen up. So why not use this as your own personal way of loosening up. Or use it as a group activity if you have the chance. Try to make up your own silly walk. Get as creative as you can and don't be afraid to show off your walk to a friend, family member, or spouse. Get them to create their own. Have fun with this.

Captionless Cartoons

Pick a few cartoons from any source (newspaper, magazine. cartoon book etc.) and remove their captions. Then come up with as many of your own captions as you can. This is great fun and a good mind stretch too.

Totally Useless Skills

I first had the pleasure of seeing Rick Davis when he did a presentation at a Humor Conference in Saratoga, New York. I have often used some of the skills I learned from Rick as diversions in my own workshops. These *include disappearing body parts, arm stretching, two noses, yodeling, spoon hanging* and many others. Sound intriguing? These activities are a great deal of fun and, more importantly, can really get people to free up some new thinking. You can find his book, Totally Useless Office Skills, on Amazon.com.

Dumb Questions

Of course, when you come right down to it, there is no such thing as a dumb question. But your object is to find some anyway. Key in on a topic, an object, a statement, or just about anything that comes to mind.

Then come up with as many dumb questions as you can regarding this item. Sound ridiculous? It is. Welcome to my world. This should create some good fodder for laughter.

Make Up a New Language

This is a blast! You almost need to try it with a close friend or friends to get the most out of it. Simply spend some time conversing in a language you make up. See if you can get a point across using this new language. You may surprise yourself! Flower it up with some good non-verbal stuff. You may even find your friends understand you better with your new language.

Silly Words

Make up a few silly words, and then try to figure out what they are, or what they mean. Here are a few to get you started:

Fratigumptuous	Forceptitute
Paridigamial	illuspronatural
Valumanian	rampithcrate
Skreeter	harmplot
Thinkamut	pesstumb
Transqualimation	kagnst
Microsoftie	bleesh

Some of you may be old enough to remember the word coined by Rich Hall, *Sniglets,* from the 80's. These were words that should be in the dictionary, but aren't. For example:

Hozone - The place where one sock in every laundry load disappears to.
Expressholes - People who try to sneak more than "8 items or less" into the express checkout line.
Fenderbergs - The large glacial deposits that form on the insides of car fenders during snowstorms.
Porkus Non Gratis - The scraggly piece of bacon at the bottom of the package.

So another form of this exercise might be to pick an object or activity and identify some *sniglets* of your own. I'd love to hear what you come up with. I can always be reached at lindsaycollier@comcast.net.

Have Your Own *'Whine and Jeez'* Party

Whining has a bad name, but might be one of the best ways you have to let off some negative steam. In my days as a Creative Process Consultant, I used a form of this exercise often. After five or ten minutes of loud, unabashed, serious whining you'll feel better, and have an open channel for some new thinking. You could do this alone, but it may be best to do it with some good friends or family.

Just spend a few minutes whining about anything you can think of, and listening to your friends whine. Then cut it off, stop your whining, and have some laughs. Need some things to whine about? Here are a few to get you started

- politics

- taxes
- rich people
- TV adds
- sports salaries
- beige Buicks
- neighbors

Stupid Questions

In the mid-eighties, *The Book of Questions* by Gregory Stock was a popular mini-book series which contained a number of rather serious questions designed to create group dialogue. A follow up spoof called the _Book of Stupid Questions_ by Tom Weller came out shortly after that. I love this book! Here are a few examples:

- If you crossed the International Date Line on your birthday would you still get presents?
- If you found you had been mix up in the hospital as a baby, would you turn yourself in?
- Have you ever had an out of body experience? How do you know?
- What kind of hen lays extra-large eggs?
- If nothing sticks to Teflon, how do they get Teflon to stick to the pan?
- If you play your portable radio louder do the batteries wear out more quickly?
- Where does lint come from?
- Would you rather be extremely happy but not know it or be miserable and not care?
- What is your favorite toe? Why?
- Would you like to be a member of the opposite sex? Why? How do you know you're not?

- What is your favorite internal organ?
- When a fly alights on a ceiling does it do a loop or a roll to get into position?
- What happens to donut holes when you eat the donut?

Try to make up as many stupid questions as you can, and then share them with your significant other and have some laughs.

The Elizabethan Insult Kit

This might be an interesting exercise to do at family or friend gatherings. It's a rather hilarious process of insulting everyone in the group, in a fun way. that was originated by Jerry Maguire, an English teacher from Greenwood, Indiana. The purpose is to just let everyone loose for a certain amount of time so that they can insult as many of their friends as they can. This is done by merely picking at random one word from each column and using these to insult everyone you come in contact with. Be careful not to spit as you become more aggressive in this exercise – you *droning, beetle-headed, hedge-pig.*

Column 1	fobbing	mewling
bawdy	frothy	
beslobering	goatish	**Column 2**
churlish	impertinent	
craven	jarring	bat-fowling
curlish	Logger-headed	beef-witted
droning	lumpish	beetle-headed
fawning	mammering	clay-brained

crook-pated

dizzy-eyed

earth-vexing

elf-skinned

fat-kidneyed

fly-bitten

fool-born

gut-gripping

halk-faced

hasty-witted

hedge-born

idle-headed

fustilarian

giglet

harpy

hedge-pig

horn-beast

jolthead

Column 3

baggage

barnacle

boar-pig

canker-blossom

clotpole

dogheart

dewberry

flap-dragon

foot-licker

Ugly Faces

A lot of us are much too serious about life, and also about needing to look good all the time. This exercise should change that, and help you release some of the ridiculousness that you possess. Instead of smiling at yourself the next time you pass by a mirror, make the ugliest face you can. Don't hold it too long because you must remember that your mother once told you that, if you did, it would stick with you. You may also try it with friends and family (who all think you are totally nuts at this point anyway).

You may want to take a few pictures of your best ugly face, and post them where they will remind you that things really aren't that serious. But why stop there? Make a monster face and walk like a monster. Hang spinach from your teeth, and see if anyone notices. I think I'm losing it here - I better take a break.

The Big Flush

Are there some things that are getting in the way, and blocking your sense of humor? Grab some toilet paper, and write these down. Then take a careful look at them, go to the nearest bathroom, and flush them right down the toilet. Say goodbye, and have a good laugh.

If you don't feel like flushing them then have a small bonfire, shred them, write them on something edible (like a candy bar), and eat them.

Silly Handshakes/Greetings

Always greet everyone with a smile but, when it comes time for a handshake, or other form of greeting, try something different. Make up a few strange and silly handshakes and other forms of greeting, and try them out from time to time with friends. Have them collaborate with you on this and make up their own.

Try Out Some of Those Totally Useless Skills

Earlier, I mentioned the book, *Totally Useless Skills*. Go to Amazon.com right now and order this book if you'd like to develop some of these skills. Or perhaps you already have some of your own useless skills. Some people are good at balancing spoons on their nose. And if you happen to be one of these incredibly talented people, do it often. Impress your friends, or yourself in the mirror. Wet a nickel with your tongue and press it on your forehead, and see how long it stays. Have contests with friends to see whose stays the longest.

Or try to see how smart your right foot is. Lift your right foot off the floor and make clockwise circles with it. While doing this, draw the number '6' in the air with your right hand. Your foot will then change direction. And, there is nothing you can do about it! Keep on trying Give me a call if you can keep this from happening.

You may want to search the internet for more of these activities, or just go ahead and invent some of your own.

Turning Up Your Smile Volume

Stand in front of a mirror and give yourself a slight smirk. Turn that smirk into a bit of a grin, and then increase the size of this grin until the edges of your mouth meet your ears. Turn this into a smile and raise the level this smile until it hurts. Chuckle for a while, and then laugh lightly, and raise that laugh slowly to a belly laugh. See if you can laugh until you cry. Try not to hurt yourself.

Practice Your Happy Words

Put together a few sentences using as many happy words (see Appendix 3) as you can. It might be best to do this early in your day, and use sentences that relate to your planned day's activities. This will start you out with a positive focus.

There's a few to get you started. Go ahead and invent some new ones. and have a lot of fun doing it. Let me know what you come up with.

Chapter 6

Let's Put it All Together; A Ten Day Program to Supercharge Your Humor

Every smile makes you a day younger. —*Chinese Proverb*

At this point, I hope you have soaked up a lot of good information and ideas about the importance of humor in your life, and how to access your own sense of humor. Many of you undoubtedly have well-developed funny bones. And there are likely some of you who, for a variety of reasons, have some difficulty accessing your humor. Where would you put yourself on a scale of 1-10 on your ability to use humor in your life? If you are a '10', you begin each day with smile, and end it with a laugh. And all those you come in contact with do too. If you are a '1', the last time you smiled or laughed was when you had gas as a child.

I am going to leave you with a ten-day program to help you build up your humor potential. No matter what your present state is in terms of your ability to fully access your sense of humor, you should give this program a try. For each day, I've listed seven tasks for you to do. Why seven? Seven is a lucky number, and there are seven habits, wonders, pillars, deadly sins, and more. It's worked in the past so I think it will work for you. Feel free to put your own spin on any of these suggestions.

Check off the items as you complete them . It will make you feel good. Have fun!

Day One

- ○ Start your day by standing tall, taking a deep breath, and flashing a big smile. Find a mirror, and flash a big smile to whoever you see in it.

- ○ Get on your computer, IPod, Smartphone, or other favorite device, and Google "Baby Laughing at Ripping Paper". This should give you a good "kick start". Watch it several times.

o Go to your local bookstore and check out the books in the humor section. Buy a David Barry book (see my suggestions in Appendix 4).

o Find a folder and label it "My Silly File". Find at least one thing that strikes you funny, and put it in your file. File it in front of your "bills to be paid" file.

o Using the old adage that, "you are what you think", concentrate on thinking of yourself as the funniest person you know.

o Give your best smile to at last 3 people today.

o Stand, breath, and smile just before going to bed.

Day Two

o Before you get out of bed, think about two instances in your life that really tickled your funny bone, and make them your "smile mindsets". Imbed the first one on your right index finger, and the second on your nose. Practice squeezing your finger and nose to bring these up.

o Start with a stand, breath, and smile. Then find a mirror a flash yourself a big smile.

o Be on the lookout for people you see smiling. Tell them they have a nice smile.

o Look over the quotations in Appendix 1, and pick one or two that inspire you. Put these on your email signature, answering machine message, car visor, or any other place that you see often.

o Look for at least 3 things to put in your "Silly File" folder. If you are somewhat computer savvy, set up a folder on your

PC, and call it your "Silly File". If you have Microsoft Word or an equivalent, create your silly file as a document. Then Google "silly stuff' and find at least three things that you can cut and paste to your file. Feel free to use any of the snippets I've included in Appendix 2. Send me an email at lindsaycollier@comcast.net, and I'll send you back a document that you can copy and paste to your file.

o Make a list of your friends, associates, and family members who have the best sense of humor. Make a resolution to spend more time with them.

o Just before you go to bed, find one of your favorite comedians in Appendix 4, and listen to one or two of their YouTubes. I suggest you begin with Foster Brooks as a Brain Surgeon.

Day Three

o Before you get out of bed, squeeze your nose, and your index finger to see if your two smile mindsets come up. Spend a little time with these happy thoughts.

o Arise, and start with a stand, breath, and smile. Then, take a deep breath, and *howl like a wolf.* End with a smile and a loud chuckle.

o Find a mirror and make the ugliest face you can to whoever appears in front of you.

o Make it a point to smile and say a friendly "hello" to at least four strangers today.

o Find some "happy stuff" to decorate your office, den, and any other place where you tend to spend time.

- Make it a point to smile during every phone conversation today.

- Before retiring check out at least three Dean Martin Roasts on YouTube.

Day Four

- Stand, take a deep breath, and laugh as loud as you can. Try not to wake up the whole neighborhood.

- Add a few things to both your digital, and hard copy "Silly Files".

- Greet and smile at as many people as possible today.

- Carefully observe your surroundings during the day, and identify some things you found funny. If you have trouble finding things that are funny, then find ways to make them funny. Practice your ability to be a "glutton for funishment".

- Check out The Ministry of Silly Walks on YouTube. Make up your own silly walk, and practice it a few times today. Invite someone close to you to be a part of this silly walk if you can.

- Sit down and make a list of all the things that make you sad, or unhappy, or just bother you in some way. Get a roll of toilet paper, write down these things, and flush them. An alternative is to wad them up and put them in your mouth. Then have someone perform a mock Heimlich Maneuver on you, and spit them out.

o Watch one of the movies listed in Appendix 7. Substitute your favorite funny movie if it's not listed.

Day Five

o Stand, breath, and smile with someone you love.

o Watch the baby laughing video again, and check out some of the other ones too. If you can, try to observe some children at play. Remember what it was like when you were a child playing? Think of some things you can do to get that feeling back. Remember, it's never too late to have a happy childhood.

o Think of a couple of your favorite jokes, and tell them to some friends. If you can't remember any, then go to the internet and find some. You can also find some really good ones in Appendix 2. Commit a few to your memory.

o If you receive a daily paper, go through the Comics section and select at least three that you want to check out on a daily basis (mine are Dilbert, Frank and Ernest, and Mallard Fillmore). That doesn't mean you have to limit yourself to three, though. If you are not a daily paper reader, go to gocomics.com, and find some you like there. Either way, try to make this a daily habit.

o Call a few of your best friends just to say "Hi", and see how they are doing. Do you have some friends you haven't spoken to in ages? Consider calling some of them too. Smile throughout the conversation, and use as many happy words as you can while you are on the phone with them.

- Check to see if your "Smile Mindsets" are still where you left them. Try to think of another one, and imbed that in one of your ears.

- Before retiring, make a few ugly faces at yourself in the mirror, and then the biggest smile possible. Try to have the edges of your mouth meet your ears when you smile.

Day Six

- Start your day by standing, taking a deep breath, and then raising your humor level. Do this by starting with a slight grin, turning into an ever-increasing smile, then a chuckle, a laugh. and a belly laugh. Again, be careful not to hurt yourself.

- Find someone you want to make happy today - and make their day with your humor!

- Carry out a conversation with one of your friends in a totally new language. Really ham it up on this one and have a lot of laughs.

- Check out Appendix 5 and try at least three silly things. See if you can make up a few of your own.

- Read your Dave Barry book for at least an hour today.

- Watch another one of the funny movies shown in Appendix 7. Add any other of your funny movies to the list, and make a pact with yourself to watch at least one per week.

o   Visit a couple of the humor websites in Appendix 6, and wander around. Google some humor related words, and see if you can find some more sites. Bookmark these sites and make a habit of visiting them often.

Day Seven

o   Start your day with a stand, breathe , and smile in front of a mirror. Put a bit of a different spin on it this time . Begin with a grin, then a smirk, then a chuckle, and then an ever-widening smile.

o   Find some cartoons and remove their captions. Come up with as many funny captions for these as you can. Share these with a friend.

o   Go to Smile on a Stick and order a few smile sticks.

o   Check out your "Smile Mindsets" to see if they come up. Remember, at this point you have embedded one in your index finger, one in your nose, and one in your ear. Squeezing the appropriate spot should bring them up. Let these thoughts make your day.

o   Have a "Whine and Jeez" party with some friends. Spend at least seven minutes whining about anything you can think of. Then have a few laughs and forget about it.

o   Check out Appendix 2 (Snippets from my Silly File) and share one or two of the jokes here with some of your friends.

o   Smile at everyone you meet today. Tell those who return your smile how nice a smile they have.

Day Eight

o Wander around, and see how many things you can find that are humorous, or that you can turn into humorous. Pat yourself on the back, and congratulate yourself on becoming a talented "Glutton For Funishment".

o Look for a Laughter Yoga Club in your area and make arrangements to attend their next meeting. If you can't find one, think about starting one.

o Go to your local bookstore again, and visit the humor section. Buy a couple of books that sound appealing, and set aside some time to read them.

o Tickle someone's funny bone today. See if you can make someone smile and laugh. Challenge yourself, and pick a person you know who rarely smiles or laughs.

o Find another comedian in Appendix 4, and watch their YouTube videos.

o Add a few more humorous quotations to your surroundings.

o Just before you go to sleep, bring up your "Smile Mindsets", and bring yourself back to those funny moments in your life. Cherish these thoughts, and fall asleep thinking bout them.

Day Nine

o   Wake up to the thoughts of the "Smile Mindsets" you went to sleep thinking about. Try to keep those thoughts with you throughout the day.

o   Share one or two of the items from Appendix 2 with some friends.

o   Look over the happy words in Appendix 3. Use as many of these as you can in today's conversations.

o   Visit several of the humorous websites in Appendix 6, and wander around.

o   Check out your "Silly Files", and find a bunch of new items for them. Plan on how you will make this a habit in your life.

o   Identify some really silly metaphors for your life. Complete the sentence, "Why is my life like a _____?" Have fun with this one, and see what messages are contained in the statements.

o   Make an affirmation before retiring tonight that you will continue to make humor a major part of your life. Fall asleep repeating this to yourself.

Day Ten - Graduation Day!!

o   Look in the mirror, smile, howl like a wolf, make an ugly face, and laugh heartily at yourself. This is graduation day. Think of yourself wearing a graduation gown adorned with smiley faces.

- o Spend the good part of an hour juicing up your "Silly File". Then go through it, and have some laughs.

- o Smile at everyone today and look for opportunities to share some things from your "Silly File".

- o Read a chapter or two of your Dave Barry Book.

- o Focus on your happy words and use them as much as you can.

- o Take your best friend or spouse to see a funny movie.

- o Before going to bed, reaffirm the promise to yourself to continue to build on your wonderful sense of humor.

Congratulations. Take yourself out to eat with your significant other. Laugh and smile all night. Make an affirmation to yourself that you will continue to make humor a major part of your life.

I've had a wonderful time writing this book. But, what really excites me is knowing that this book may create a positive change in so many lives. I sincerely hope you are one of those folks. My best to you !

But wait - there's more! The following Appendix is loaded with some great humor stuff. It's a real blast! Have fun!

Appendix

Following is some really great *humor fodder* to help you along the way. If you would like *Word* copies of any of these, just send me an email at lindsaycollier@comcast.net, let me know what you want, and I'll send it right to you. That's just the type of guy I am!

Appendix 1 - Smile Quotes

The following is a chunk of my collection of quotations dealing with humor and laughter. Quotations can be very inspirational. As you look over these, think of what it might mean to you in terms of making humor a major part of your life. if I haven't included the author, its either anonymous or unknown.

One of my other books, **Quotations to Tickle Your Brain**, contains some of the greatest quotes to stimulate your creative thinking. You should have a copy of this in every bathroom.

After every storm the sun will smile; for every problem there is a solution, and the soul's indefeasible duty is to be of good cheer. – William R. Alger

You're never fully dressed without a smile. – Martin Charnin

A smile is happiness you'll find right under your nose. – Tom Wilson

"I was smiling yesterday, I am smiling today, and I will smile tomorrow. Simply because life is too short to cry for anything." - Santosh Kalwar

Remember even though the outside world might be raining, if you keep on smiling, the sun will soon show its face and smile back at you. – Anna Lee

"Sometimes your joy is the source of your smile, but sometimes your smile can be the source of your joy." - Thich Nhat Hanh

When I look out at the people, and they look at me, and they're smiling, then I know that I'm loved. That is the time when I have no worries, no problems. – Etta James

A well-developed sense of humor is the pole that adds balance to your steps as you walk the tightrope of life. – William Arthur Ward

If I had no sense of humor, I would long ago have committed suicide. – Gandhi

The world always looks brighter from behind a smile.

Always remember to be happy because you never know who's falling in love with your smile.

"If I can see pain in your eyes, then share with me your tears. If I can see joy in your eyes, then share with me your smile." - Santosh Kalwar

Use your smile to change the world; don't let the world change your smile.

Never regret something that once made you smile.

You are somebody's reason to smile.

The more I live, the more I think that humor is the saving sense. – Jacob August Riis

Humor is mankind's greatest blessing. - Mark Twain

Every smile makes you a day younger. - Chinese Proverb

Seven days without laughter make one weak.

The secret source of humor itself is not joy, but sorrow. – Mark Twain

Do not take life seriously. You'll never get out of it alive.

People do not quit playing because they get old. They get old because they quite playing.

Laughter is like changing a baby's diaper. It doesn't change things permanently but it makes it better for a while.

The real happy person is the one who can enjoy the scenery on a detour.

It's never too late to have a happy childhood. You are only young once, but you can be immature all your life

Laughter is the shock absorber that eases the blows of life.

Those who bring sunshine into the lives of others cannot keep it from themselves.

Some people grin and bear it. Others smile and change it.

Laughter is the shortest distance between two people. - Victor Borge

There is no cosmetic for beauty like happiness. - Lady Blessington

With the fearful strain that is on me night and day, if I did not laugh, I should die. – Abraham Lincoln

A day without laughter is a day wasted.-Charlie Chaplin

The greatest part of our happiness depends on our dispositions, not our circumstances. – Martha Washington

Smile, it improves your face value.

*A person without a sense of humor is like a wagon without springs –
jolted by every pebble on the road – Henry Ward Beecher*

*I think the next best thing to solving a problem is finding some
humor in it. – Frank Howard Clark*

*Your body can't heal without play. Your mind cannot heal without
laughter. Your soul can't heal without joy. - Catherine Rippenger
Fenwick*

Appendix 2 - Snippets From My Silly File

A few of my favorite Jokes:

Italian chocolate

An Irishman and an Italian entered a chocolate store. As they were busy looking, the Irishman stole three chocolate bars.
As they left the store, the Irishman said to the Italian, "Man I'm the best thief. I stole three chocolate bars and no one saw me. You can't beat that."

The Italian said, "You want to see something better? Let's go back to the shop and I'll show you real stealing."So they went to the counter, and the Italian said to the shopkeeper, "Do you want to see magic?"

The shopkeeper replied, "Yes." The Italian said, "Give me one chocolate bar." The shopkeeper gave him one, and he ate it. The Italian asked for a second bar, and he ate that as well. Then he asked for the third, and finished that one too.

The shopkeeper asked, "But where's the magic?"

The Italian replied, "Check in my friend's pocket, and you'll find all three chocolate bars."

Leroy from Detroit

In a Detroit church one Sunday morning, a preacher said, "Anyone with *special needs* who wants to be prayed over, please come forward to the front by the altar." With that, Leroy got in line, and when it was his turn, the Preacher asked, "Leroy, what do you want me to pray about for you?" Leroy replied, "Preacher, I need you to pray for help with my hearing."

The preacher put one finger of one hand on Leroy's ear, placed his other hand on top of Leroy's head, and then prayed, and prayed, and prayed. He prayed a "blue streak" for Leroy, and the whole congregation joined in with great enthusiasm.

After a few minutes, the preacher removed his hands, stood back and asked, "Leroy, how is your hearing now?" Leroy answered, "I don't know. It ain't 'til Thursday."

The priest, minister and rabbi

A Catholic Priest, a Southern Baptist Preacher and a Rabbi all served as Chaplains to the students of Northern Michigan University at Marquette in the Upper Peninsula of Michigan. They would get together two or three times a week for coffee and to talk shop. One day, someone made the comment that preaching to people isn't really all that hard, a real challenge would be to preach to a bear. One thing led to another, and they decided to do an experiment. They would all go out into the woods, find a bear, preach to it, and attempt to convert it to their religion.

Seven days later, they got together to discuss their experiences. Father Flannery, who had his arm in a sling, was on crutches, and had various bandages on his body and limbs, went first. "Well," he said, "I went into the woods to find a bear. And when I found him, I began to read to him from my Catechism. Well, that bear wanted nothing to do with me and began to slap me around. So I grabbed my holy water bottle, sprinkled him and, Holy Mary Mother of God, he became as gentle as a lamb. The Bishop is coming out next week to give him first communion and confirmation."

Reverend Billy Bob, the Sothern Baptist spoke next. He was in a wheelchair, had one arm and both legs in casts. In his best fire-and-brimstone oratory, he exclaimed, 'WELL, brothers, you KNOW that we Baptists don't sprinkle holy water! I went out and I FOUND a bear. And then I began to read to the bear from God's HOLY WORD! But that bear wanted nothing to do with me. So I took HOLD of him and we began to wrestle. We wrestled down the hill until we came to a creek. So I quickly DUNKED him and BAPTIZED his hairy soul. And just like you said, he became as gentle as a lamb. We spent the rest of the day praising Jesus. Hallelujah! "

The Priest and the Reverend both looked down at the Rabbi, who was lying in bed in a body cast and traction with IVs and monitors running in and out of him. He was in really bad shape. The Rabbi said, "Looking back on it, circumcision may not have been the best way to start."

The best drunk story

A drunk walks into a biker bar, sits down at the bar and orders a drink. Looking around, he sees three men sitting at a corner table. He gets up, staggers to the table, leans over, looks the biggest, meanest, biker in the face and says, "'I went by your grandma's house today, and I saw her in the hallway buck-naked. Man, she is one fine looking woman!"

The biker looks at him and doesn't say a word. His buddies are confused, because he is one bad biker, and would fight at the drop of a hat. The drunk leans on the table again and says, "I got it on with your grandma, and she is good, the best I ever had!"

The biker's buddies are starting to get really mad but the biker still says nothing. The drunk leans on the table one more time and says, "I'll tell you something else, boy, your grandma liked it!"

At this point the biker stands up, takes the drunk by the shoulders, looks him square in the eyes and says.................. '

Grandpa, go home!'

The man and wife at the dentist

A man and his wife walked into a dentist's office. The man said to the dentist, "Doc, I'm in one heck of a hurry. I have two buddies sitting out in my car waiting for us to go play golf, so forget about the anesthetic, I don't have time for the gums to get numb. I just want you to pull the tooth, and be done with it! We have a 10:00 AM tee time at the best golf course in town and it's 9:30 already. I don't have time to wait for the anesthetic to work!'

The dentist thought to himself, "My goodness, this is surely a very brave man asking to have his tooth pulled without using anything to kill the pain." So the dentist asks him, "Which tooth is it sir?"

The man turned to his wife and said, "Open your mouth, Honey, and show him."

Two old guys

Two 90-year-old men, Phil and Joe, had been friends all of their lives. When it was clear that Phil was dying, Joe visited him every day. One day Joe said, "Phil, we both loved playing baseball all our lives, and we played all through high school. Please do me one favor - when you get to heaven, somehow you must let me know if there's baseball there."
Phil looked up at Joe from his deathbed and said, "Joe, you've been

my best friend for many years. If it's at all possible, I'll do this favor for you." Shortly after that, Phil died.

A few nights later, Joe was awakened from a sound sleep by a blinding flash of white light and a voice calling out to him, "Joe, Joe." "Who is it," asked Joe, sitting up suddenly. "Who is it?" 'Joe -- it's me, Phil". "You're not Phil. Phil just died." "I'm telling you, it's me, Phil," insisted the voice.

"Phil Where are you?" "In heaven," replied Phil. "I have some really good news and a little bad news." "Tell me the good news first," said Joe. "The good news," Phil said with joy and enthusiasm, "is that there is baseball in heaven. Better yet, all of our old buddies who died before me are here too. Even better than that, we're all young again. Better still, it's always springtime and it never rains or snows. And best of all, we can play ball all we want, and we never get tired. And we get to play with all the Greats of the past". "That's fantastic," said Joe "It's beyond my wildest dreams! So what's the bad news?"

"You're pitching Tuesday."

The Florida senior citizen

A Florida senior citizen drove his brand new Corvette convertible out of the dealership. Taking off down the road, he pushed it to 80 mph, enjoying the wind blowing through what little hair he had left. "Amazing," he thought as he flew down I-95, pushing the pedal even more.

Looking in his rear view mirror, he saw a Florida State Trooper, blue lights flashing, and siren blaring. He floored it to 100 mph, then 110, then 120. Suddenly he thought, "What am I doing? I'm too old for this!" and pulled over to await the trooper's arrival.

Pulling in behind him, the trooper got out of his vehicle and walked up to the Corvette. He looked at his watch, then said, "Sir, my shift ends in 30 minutes. Today is Friday. If you can give me a new reason for speeding – a reason I've never before heard – I'll let you go."

The old gentleman paused then said, "Three years ago, my wife ran off with a Florida State Trooper. I thought you were bringing her back.

"Have a good day, Sir," replied the trooper.

Old couple getting married

Jacob, age 92, and **Mary**, age 89, living in The Villages, are all excited about their decision to get married. They go for a stroll to discuss the wedding, and on the way they pass a drugstore. Jacob suggests they go in. Jacob addresses the man behind the counter:

"Are you the owner?" The pharmacist answers, "Yes."

Jacob: "We're about to get married. Do you sell heart medication?"
Pharmacist: "Of course we do."
Jacob: "How about medicine for circulation?"
Pharmacist: "All kinds."
Jacob: "Medicine for rheumatism?"
Pharmacist: "Definitely."
Jacob: "How about suppositories and medicine for impotence?"
Pharmacist: "You bet!"
Jacob: "Medicine for memory problems, arthritis and Alzheimer's?"
Pharmacist: "Yes, a large variety. The works."
Jacob: "What about vitamins, sleeping pills, Geritol, antidotes for Parkinson's disease?"
Pharmacist: "Absolutely."
Jacob: "Everything for heartburn and indigestion?"

Pharmacist: "We sure do."

Jacob: "You sell wheelchairs and walkers and canes?"

Pharmacist: "All speeds and sizes."

Jacob: "Adult diapers?"

Pharmacist: "Sure."

Jacob: "We'd like to use this store as our Bridal Registry."

The FBI assassination test

The FBI had an opening for an assassin. After all the background checks, interviews and testing were done, there were 3 finalists; two men and a woman.

For the final test, the FBI agents took one of the men to a large metal door and handed him a gun. "We must know that you will follow your instructions no matter what the circumstances. Inside the room you will find your wife sitting in a chair. Kill her!!"

The man said, "You can't be serious. I could never shoot my wife." The agent said, "Then you're not the right man for this job. Take your wife and go home." The second man was given the same instructions. He took the gun and went into the room. All was quiet for about 5 minutes. The man came out with tears in his eyes, "I tried, but I can't kill my wife.'" The agent said, "You don't have what it takes. Take your wife and go home."

Finally, it was the woman's turn. She was given the same instructions, to kill her husband. She took the gun and went into the room. Shots were heard, one after another. They heard screaming, crashing, banging on the walls. After a few minutes, all was quiet. The door opened slowly, and there stood the woman, wiping the sweat from her brow.

"This gun is loaded with blanks," she said. "I had to beat him to death with the chair."

The elderly Italian's confession

An elderly Italian man who lived on the outskirts of Rimini, Italy, went to the local church for confession. When the priest slid open the panel in the confessional, the man said, "Father... During World War II, a beautiful Jewish woman from our neighborhood knocked urgently on my door, and asked me to hide her from the Nazis. So I hid her in my attic." The priest replied, "That was a wonderful thing you did, and you have no need to confess that." "There is more to tell, Father. She started to repay me with sexual favors. This happened several times a week, and sometimes twice on Sundays." The priest said, "That was a long time ago and by doing what you did, you placed the two of you in great danger, but two people under those circumstances can easily succumb to the weakness of the flesh. However, if you are truly sorry for your actions, you are indeed forgiven." "Thank you, Father. That's a great load off my mind. I do have one more question." "And what is that?" asked the priest.

"Should I tell her the war is over?"

The old guy's will

An aging man had serious hearing problems for a number of years. He went to the doctor, and the doctor was able to have him fitted for a set of hearing aids that allowed the gentleman to hear 100% The elderly gentleman went back in a month to the doctor and the doctor said, "Your hearing is perfect. Your family must be really pleased that you can hear again."
The gentleman replied, "Oh, I haven't told my family yet.
I just sit around and listen to the conversations. I've changed my will three times!'"

The old guy's memory

An elderly couple had dinner at another couple's house, and after eating, the wives left the table and went into the kitchen.

The two gentlemen were talking, and one said, "Last night we went out to a new restaurant and it was really great. I would recommend it very highly."

The other man said, "What is the name of the restaurant?"

The first man thought and thought and finally said, "What is the name of that flower you give to someone you love? You know... The one that's red and has thorns."

"Do you mean a rose?"

"Yes, that's the one," replied the man. He then turned towards the kitchen and yelled, "Rose, what's the name of that restaurant we went to last night?"

Hospital regulations

Hospital regulations require a wheel chair for patients being discharged. However, while working as a student nurse, I found one elderly gentleman already dressed and sitting on the bed with a suitcase at his feet who insisted he didn't need my help to leave the hospital.

After a chat about rules being rules, he reluctantly let me wheel him to the elevator. On the way down I asked him if his wife was meeting him. "I don't know," he said. "She's still upstairs in the bathroom changing out of her hospital gown.'"

Memory problems

Couple in their nineties are both having problems remembering things. During a checkup, the doctor tells them that they're physically okay, but they might want to start writing things down to help them remember. Later that night, while watching TV, the old man gets up from his chair. "Want anything while I'm in the kitchen?" he asks. "Will you get me a bowl of ice cream?" "Sure." "Don't you think you should write it down so you can remember it?" she asks. "No, I can remember it."
"Well, I'd like some strawberries on top, too. Maybe you should write it down, so you don't forget it?"
He says, "I can remember that. You want a bowl of ice cream with strawberries."
"I'd also like whipped cream. I'm certain you'll forget that, write it down." Irritated, he says, "I don't need to write it down, I can remember it! Ice cream with strawberries and whipped cream - I got it, for goodness sake!'"
Then he toddles into the kitchen. After about 20 minutes, the old man returns from the kitchen, and hands his wife a plate of bacon and eggs. She stares at the plate for a moment and says, "Where's my toast?'

Three old guys

Three old guys are out walking.
First one says, "Windy, isn't it?"
Second one says, "No, it's Thursday!'"
Third one says, "So am I. Let's go get a beer."

Morris' exam

Morris, an 82 year-old man, went to the doctor to get a physical.
A few days later, the doctor saw Morris walking down the street
with a gorgeous young woman on his arm.
A couple of days later, the doctor spoke to Morris and said, "You're
really doing great, aren't you?"
Morris replied, "Just doing what you said, Doc, to get a hot mamma
and be cheerful."
The doctor said, "I didn't say that. I told you you've got a heart
murmur and to be careful.'

And here are a few other oddball snippets:

Ten Best Caddy Responses

Number :10
Golfer: "I think I'm going to drown myself in the
lake."
Caddy: "Think you can keep your head down that
long?"

Number : 9
Golfer: "I'd move heaven and earth to break 100 on
this course."
Caddy: "Try heaven, you've already moved most of
the earth."

Number : 8
Golfer: "Do you think my game is improving?"
Caddy: "Yes . . . . You miss the ball much closer

now."

Number : 7
Golfer: "Do you think I can get there with a 5 iron?"
Caddy: "Eventually."

Number : 6
Golfer: "You've got to be the worst caddy in the world."
Caddy: "I don't think so . . . .That would be too much of a coincidence."

Number : 5
Golfer: "Please stop checking your watch all the time. It's too much of a distraction."
Caddy: "It's not a watch - it's a compass."

Number : 4
Golfer: "How do you like my game?"
Caddy: "It's very good - but personally, I prefer golf."

Number : 3
Golfer: "Do you think it's a sin to play on Sunday?
Caddy: "The way you play, it's a sin on any day."

Number : 2
Golfer: "This is the worst course I've ever played on."
Caddy: "This isn't the golf course . . . . We left that an hour ago."

And the Number : 1 . . . . Best Caddy Comment:
Golfer: "That can't be my ball, it's too old."
Caddy: "It's been a long time since we teed off, sir."

Football Season is Here!

Urban Meyer on one of his players:

> "He doesn't know the meaning of the word fear. In fact, I just saw his grades and he doesn't know the meaning of a lot of words."

Why do Tennessee fans wear orange?

> So they can dress that way for the game on Saturday, go hunting on Sunday, and pick up trash on Monday.

What does the average Alabama player get on his SATs?

> Drool.

How many Ohio State freshmen football players does it take to change a light bulb?

> None. That's a sophomore course.

How did the Georgia football player die from drinking milk?

> The cow fell on him.

Two West Virginia football players were walking in the woods.

> One of them said, "Look, a dead bird." The other looked up in the sky and said, "Where?"

A Notre Dame University football player was almost killed yesterday in a tragic horseback-riding accident. He fell from a horse and was nearly trampled to death. Luckily, the manager of the Wal-Mart came out and unplugged the horse.

What do you say to a Michigan State University football player dressed in a three-piece suit? "

> "Will the defendant please rise."

If three Florida State football players are in the same car, who is driving?

The police officer.

How can you tell if an Auburn football player has a girlfriend?

There's tobacco juice on both sides of the pickup truck.

What do you get when you put 32 Arkansas cheerleaders in one room?

A full set of teeth.

University of Michigan Coach Brady Hoke is only going to dress half of his players for the game this week; the other half will have to dress themselves.

How is the Indiana football team like an opossum?

They play dead at home and get killed on the road.

Why did the Texas linebacker steal a police car?

He saw "911" on the side and thought it was a Porsche.

How do you get a former Illinois football player off your porch?

Pay him for the pizza.

'OLD' IS WHEN...

Your sweetie says, "Let's go upstairs and make love," and you answer, "Pick one; I can't do both!"

Your friends compliment you on your new alligator shoes, and you're barefoot.

A sexy babe or hunk catches your fancy and your pacemaker opens the garage door.

Going braless pulls all the wrinkles out of your face.

You are cautioned to slow down by the doctor instead of by the police.

'Getting lucky' means you find your car in the parking lot.

An 'all nighter' means not getting up to use the bathroom.

Cigar Insurance

Here is a short article I saw in the paper a while back:

Without honesty, karma has a funny way of catching up. Consider the cigar smoker who purchased several hundred expensive stogies and had them insured against fire. After he smoked them, he filed a claim pointing out that they had indeed been destroyed by fire.

The insurance company refused to pay, so the man sued. The judge ruled in the man's favor saying that the cigars had indeed been insured against, and been destroyed by fire. So the insurance company paid the claim and, when the man accepted the money, promptly had him arrested for arson.

Appendix 3 – Happy Words

Here are some happy words to get your started. Try to use these in your everyday conversations. Replace any sad words you feel coming on with these. See how good it makes you feel and notice the positive impact it has on people in your conversations.

Accomplished	Caringly	Distinguished
Adored	Celebratory	Dotingly
Affectionate	Charmed	Ducky
Agreeable	Cheerful	Ebullient
Alive	Cheery	Ecstatic
Altruistic	Chipper	Effervescent
Amazed	Chirpy	Elated
Animated	Comfortable	Endeared
Beautiful	Confident	Energetic
Blameless	Content	Enjoyable
Blessed	Contented	Enlightened
Blissful	Contentment	Enthusiastic
Bouncy	Creative	Entrusted
Brave	Decent	Euphoric
Brilliant	Delighted	Excellent
Bubbly	Delightful	Exceptional
Buoyant	Determined	Excited
Calm	Dignified	Extraordinary

Exuberant

Exultant

Fabulous

Fantabulous

Fantastic

Festive

First-class

First-rate

Flattered

Fondly

Fortunate

Friendly

Fulfillment

Full of beans

Full of brio

Full of joie de vivre

Full of life

Fun-loving

Gallant

Giddy

Giggly

Glad

Gleeful

Good

Good-humored

Grateful

Gratification

Great

Greetings

Happiness

Happy

Harmonious

Heart warming

Heavenly

Helpful

High-spirited

Honest

Honorable

Honored

Hopeful

Idyllic

Impressed

In high spirits

Inspired

Invigorated

Jolly

Jovial

Joy

Joyful

Joyous

Jubilant

Just

Kind

LikingLively

Lofty

Loved

Lovely

Lovingly

Loyal

Magnificent

Marvelous

Merry

Noble

On cloud nine

Optimistic

Outstanding

Overjoyed

Peaceful

Perfect

Playful

Pleasant

Recharged

Re-energized

Refreshed

Rejuvenated

Relaxed

Respectable

Revitalized

Revived

Righteous

Romantic

Satisfaction

Warm hearted

Wholeheartedly

Well

Wonder struck

Wonderful

Pleased

Pleasurable

Pleasure

Satisfied

Smitten

Special

Spectacular

Spirited

Stoked

Successful

Superb

Sweet

Tenderly

Thankful

Privileged

Productive

Quality

Thrilled

Tickled

Touched

Tranquil

Tremendous

Triumphant

Uplifting

Victorious

Virtuous

Vivacious

Appendix 4 – The Funniest People Ever

Here is my list of some of the greatest comics I've ever known. I've included a few YouTube's and quotes just to whet your appetite. My suggestion to you is to spend some time searching the web for more material on these, and other favorites of yours. If this doesn't tickle your funny bone, nothing will! By the way, did you know that Charly Chaplin once entered a Charly Chaplin lookalike contest, and came in third?

Rowan Atkinson (Mr. Bean)

I love Mr. Bean. He's a great example of British humor, which I think is quite different. Some people, like my wife, just think it's stupid. So, what's wrong with stupid? Here are a few examples

Mr. Bean Late for the Dentist

Mr.Bean - The Exam

Lucille Ball

Growing up, my family would rarely miss watching the "I Love Lucy" show. A laugh a minute!

Lucy's famous chocolate scene

8 Hilarious moments of I Love Lucy

Dave Barry

Dave Barry was a syndicated columnist for the Miami Herald until 2005, and has written a whole bunch of books. These are my all-time favorite humor books, and perhaps the only ones which will make me laugh out loud while alone. You absolutely need to have a few of his books in your library! Here are some of my favorites:

- Babies and Other Hazards of Sex
- Homes and Other Black Holes
- Stay Fit and Healthy, Until You're Dead
- Claw Your Way to the Top: How to Become the Head of a Corporation in Roughly a Week
- Dave Barry's Greatest Hits
- Dave Barry Turns 40, and Dave Barry Turns 50

Go to his Amazon author page for the full listing.

Jack Benny

The Jack Benny Show was a program that those of us in the 50's through the 70's never missed. He is probably most famous for never being beyond 39 years of age. His ability to create laughter with a pregnant pause, or a single expression was his signature. There are loads of reruns of his program on YouTube, but here are a couple of short ones.

Jack Benny – Mel Blanc Classic Routine

George Burns Roasts Jack Benny

Foster Brooks

Foster was best known as the "Lovable Lush" and one of the best "roasters" ever. Here are a few of his best routines.

The Brain Surgeon

The Airline Pilot

Foster Roasts Don Rickles

George Burns

The comedy team of George Burns and Gracie Allen brought us to tears in the 60's.

George Burns and Gracie Allen Show

George Burns Roasts Jack Benny

Here are just a few on his one-liners:

First you forget names, then you forget faces. Next you forget to pull your zipper up and finally, you forget to pull it down.

I smoke 10 to 15 cigars a day, at my age I have to hold on to something.

Everything that goes up must come down. But there comes a time when not everything that's down can come up.

A good sermon should have a good beginning and a good ending, and they should be as close together as possible.

Actually, it only takes one drink to get me loaded. Trouble is, I can't remember if it's the thirteenth or fourteenth.

When I was a boy, the Dead Sea was only sick.

Sex at age 90 is like trying to shoot pool with a rope.

George Carlin

There's a ton of stuff on this comic genius but, I must warn you, a lot of it is pretty raw.

George Carlin - Top 20 Moments

George Carlin on Golf

Johnny Carson

Johnny hosted The Tonight Show for 30 years, a record that will likely never be broken.

Johnny Carson Sis Boom Bah Carnac

Johnny Carson Monologue

Cast of Carol Burnett

Why can't anyone put together a show today like *The Carol Burnett Show*? The combination of Carol along with Harvey Korman, Tin Conway, and Vicki Lawrence was absolutely hysterical. Look for some of the" best of" DVD's. Here are a couple of snippets:

Carol Burnett - No Frills Airline

Carol Burnett Show - Old Man in Surgery

Carol Burnett Show Dentist

Cast of Monty Python

This is the best of British humor - totally nuts! Here are some of the best outtakes:

Top 10 Monty Python Movie Moments

Monty Python - Dead Parrott

Monty Python - Silly Walk

Silly Olympics Sketch

Cast of SNL

Saturday Night Live has been keeping folks up on Saturday night for 30 years or so, and I have no idea where to begin with my favorite cast members. I suggest you spend some time searching the web for the best routines,and also pick up some of the Best of SNL DVDS.

My take at the best cast members includes Dana Garvey, Will Ferrell, Gilda Radner, Chris Farley, Edie Murphy, Dan Akroyd, and John Beluchi.

Top 10 Saturday Night Live Cast Members

Dana Garvey - Church Lady

Norm Crosby

Here's a guy who was a master at screwing up words.

Norm Crosby on the Dean Martin Show

Billy Crystal

Always a hoot!

Who's on First? (with Jimmy Fallon and Jerry Steinfeld)

Rodney Dangerfield

Rodney was the master at self-effacing comedy. His line, "I get no respect" will go down in history. Here are a couple of his videos, and a few of his best quips:

Rodney Dangerfield Live

Rodney Dangerfield Stand Up

My wife only has sex with me for a purpose. Last night she used me to time an egg.

Last night my wife met me at the front door. She was wearing a sexy negligee. The only trouble was, she was coming home.

A girl phoned me and said, "Come on over. There's nobody home."I went over. Nobody was home!

A hooker once told me she had a headache.

I was making love to this girl and she started crying. I said, "Are you going to hate yourself in the morning?"She said, "No, I hate myself now."

I knew a girl so ugly that she was known as a two-bagger. That's when you put a bag over your head in case the bag over her head comes off.

My wife is such a bad cook, if we leave dental floss in the kitchen the roaches hang themselves.

I'm so ugly I stuck my head out the window, and got arrested for mooning.

The other day I came home early and a guy was jogging, naked. I asked him, "Why?" He said, "Because you came home early."

My wife's such a bad cook, the dog begs for Alka-Seltzer.

I know I'm not sexy. When I put my underwear on, I can hear the Fruit-of-the- Loom guys giggling.

My wife is such a bad cook, in my house we pray after the meal.

My wife likes to talk to me during sex; last night she called me from a hotel.

I was such an ugly kid! When I played in the sandbox, the cat kept covering me up.

I could tell my parents hated me. My bath toys were a toaster, and radio.

I'm so ugly my father carried around a picture of the kid who came with his wallet.

When I was born, the doctor came into the waiting room and said to my father, "I'm sorry. We did everything we could, but he pulled through anyway."

I'm so ugly my mother had morning sickness...AFTER I was born.

I remember the time that I was kidnapped and they sent a piece of my finger to my father. He said he wanted more proof.

Once, when I was lost, I saw a policeman, and asked him to

help me find my parents. I said to him, "Do you think we'll ever find them?" He said, "I don't know kid. There's so many places they can hide."

I'm so ugly, I once worked in a pet shop, and people kept asking how big I'd get.

I went to see my doctor. "Doctor, every morning when I get up and I look in the mirror I feel like throwing up. What's wrong with me?" He said..."Nothing, your eyesight is perfect."

I went to the doctor because I'd swallowed a bottle of sleeping pills. My doctor told me to have a few drinks and get some rest.

With my old man I got no respect. I asked him, "How can I get my kite in the air?" He told me to run off a cliff.

One year they wanted to make me a poster boy - for birth control.

My uncle's dying wish was to have me sitting in his lap; he was in the electric chair

I am at the age where food has replaced sex in my life. In fact I've just had a mirror put over my kitchen table.

Jeff Foxworthy

His books and stand-up acts on Redneck humor are a riot!

Redneck Fashion Tips

Jeff Foxworthy Stand Up

Here are a few of his red neck lines. You might be a redneck if ---

The Blue Book value of your truck goes up and down depending on how much gas is in it.

You've been married three times, and still have the same in-laws.

You wonder how service stations keep their rest-rooms so clean.

Your wife's hairdo was once ruined by a ceiling fan.

The Halloween pumpkin on your porch has more teeth than your spouse.

You need one more hole punched in your card to get a freebie at the House of Tattoos.

You think loading the dishwasher means getting your wife drunk.

You take your dog for a walk, and you both use the same tree.

You come back from the dump with more than you took.

Your house doesn't have curtains, but your truck does.

You consider your license plate personalized because your father made it.

You have a complete set of salad bowls, and they all say "Cool Whip" on the side.

A tornado hits your neighborhood, and does $100,000 worth of improvements.

You've used a toilet brush to scratch your back.

You missed your 5th grade graduation because you were on jury duty.

Jim Gaffigan

He is one of the funniest contemporary comedians I know.

Jim Gaffigan - McDonalds

Bottled Water

Health Foods

Jackie Gleason

Jackie Gleason was best known as Ralph Kramden in "The Honeymooners". One of his funniest roles ever was the part of Buford T. Justice in the Smokey and the Bandit movie series.

A Tribute to Jackie Gleason

Classic Golf Scene

Bob Hope

Will there ever be someone as funny, and as giving as this guy? Here is an example of some of his great lines.

ON TURNING 70
'I still chase women, but only downhill'.

ON TURNING 80
'That's the time of your life when even your birthday suit needs pressing.'

ON TURNING 90
'You know you're getting old when the candles cost more than the cake.'

ON TURNING 100
'I don't feel old. In fact, I don't feel anything until noon. Then it's time for my nap.'

ON GIVING UP HIS EARLY CAREER, BOXING
'I ruined my hands in the ring. The referee kept stepping on them.'

ON NEVER WINNING AN OSCAR
'Welcome to the Academy Awards or, as it's called at my home, 'Passover'.

ON GOLF
'Golf is my profession. Show business is just to pay the green fees.'

ON PRESIDENTS
'I have performed for 12 presidents and entertained only six.'

ON WHY HE CHOSE SHOWBIZ FOR HIS CAREER
'When I was born, the doctor said to my mother, Congratulations, you have an eight pound ham.

ON RECEIVING THE CONGRESSIONAL GOLD MEDAL
'I feel very humble, but I think I have the strength of character to fight it.'

ON HIS FAMILY'S EARLY POVERTY
'Four of us slept in the one bed. When it got cold, mother threw on another brother.'

ON HIS SIX BROTHERS
'That's how I learned to dance. Waiting for the bathroom.'

ON HIS EARLY FAILURES
'I would not have had anything to eat if it wasn't for the stuff the audience threw at me.'

ON GOING TO HEAVEN
'I've done benefits for ALL religions. I'd hate to blow the hereafter on a technicality.'

YouTube is loaded with examples of Bob Hope but he is probably best loved for his many visits with our troops. See Bob Hope Through The Years With The Troops and you'll see what I'm talking about.

Larry the Cable Guy

Larry The Cable Guy in Pittsburgh

Larry The Cable Guy

Daniel Lawrence "Larry" Whitney, best known by his stage name and character, *Larry the Cable Guy*, is an American stand-up comedian, actor, voice actor, and former radio personality. His comedy is quite different, and he's funny as all get out! Check out these snippets.

Jay Leno

Jay Leno was a great follow-up to Johnny Cason on The Tonight Show.

Jay Leno Stand Up.

Jay Leno Headlines Also check out his books by the same name.

He loved stupid criminals - The Worlds Stupidest Criminal and 99 Cent Store Gift Ideas

Dean Martin

As a kid I remember loving the Dean Martin and Jerry Lewis show. Jerry was a little strange, but Dean had a great sense of humor. All you need to do is search for "Dean Martin Celebrity Roasts", and you'll soon be in stitches.

Bob Newhart

Bob Newhart is noted for his dead pan, slightly stammering delivery. I well remember his albums in the 60's called, *The Button Down Mind of Bob Newhart*.

The Driving Instuctor

The Police Lineup

Bob Newhart Roasts Don Rickles

Paula Poundstone

One funny lady!

Paula Poundstone Stand Up

Don Rickles

Normally I wouldn't put a comedian on this list who's major punch line is alienating people. He is a master at this, and does it in such a way that makes everyone laugh – even if they are the butt of his jokes.

Don Rickles Roast Ronald Reagan
Frank Sinatra is Surprised by Don Rickles on Johnny Carson's Show, Funniest Moment
Don Rickles Roasts Sammy Davis Jr

Joan Rivers

A sad loss way before her time.

Joan Rivers Live at The Apollo

Rita Rudner

Maybe one of the funniest comediennes ever. She just has a great style!

Rita Rudner in Las Vegas

Rita on the Johnny Carson Show

Here are a few great quotes from Rita:

I was going to have cosmetic surgery until I noticed that the doctor's office was full of portraits by Picasso.

I love being married. It's so great to find that one special person you want to annoy for the rest of your life.

I wonder if other dogs think poodles are members of a weird religious cult.

In Hollywood a marriage is a success if it outlasts milk.

I got kicked out of ballet class because I pulled a groin muscle. It wasn't mine.

Before I met my husband, I'd never fallen in love, though I'd stepped in it a few times.

I was a vegetarian until I started leaning toward the sunlight.

Most turkeys taste better the day after; my mother's tasted better the day before.

When I meet a man I ask myself, 'Is this the man I want my children to spend their weekends with?'

My mother buried three husbands, and two of them were just napping.

My husband gave me a necklace. It's fake. I requested fake. Maybe I'm paranoid, but in this day and age, I don't want something around my neck that's worth more than my head.

Red Skelton

Many of you won't remember Red Skelton. His early TV shows were watched religiously by many of us who are now in our golden years.

Here are a few of his snippets:

RED SKELTON'S RECIPE
FOR THE PERFECT MARRIAGE

- Two times a week we go to a nice restaurant, have a little beverage, good food and companionship. She goes on Tuesdays; I go on Fridays.
- We also sleep in separate beds. Hers is in California, and mine is in Texas.
- I take my wife everywhere, but she keeps finding her way back.
- I asked my wife where she wanted to go for our anniversary. "Somewhere I haven't been in a long time!" she said. So I suggested the kitchen.
- We always hold hands. If I let go, she shops.
- She has an electric blender, electric toaster and electric bread maker.
  She said "There are too many gadgets, and no place to sit down!" So I bought her an electric chair.
- My wife told me the car wasn't running well because there was water in the carburetor. I asked where the car was. She told me, "In the lake."
- She got a mud pack and looked great for two days. Then the mud fell off.
- She ran after the garbage truck, yelling, "Am I too late for the garbage?" The driver said, "No, jump in!"
- Remember: Marriage is the number one cause of divorce.
- I married Miss Right. I just didn't know her first name was 'Always'.
- I haven't spoken to my wife in 18 months. I don't like to interrupt her.
- The last fight was my fault though. My wife asked, "What's on the TV?" I said, "Dust!"

Robin Williams

A true comic genius and master of spontaneity – such a terrible loss. Here are a couple of hisYouTube's. The golf routine is one of the funniest routines I've ever seen but, warning, it can get a bit crude. There are a number his full routines on YouTube if you have some extra time.

Robin Williams - Golf

Robin Williams as the American Flag

Jonathan Winters

In my younger days I thought he was about the funniest guy ever, very much like the humor of Robin Williams. Here are a couple of examples of his humor.

Jonathan Winters and Robin Williams Improvise

Jonathan Winters and Robin Williams on Johnny Carson

Steven Wright

Steven Wright is known for his distinctively lethargic voice, and slow, deadpan delivery of ironic, philosophical, and sometimes nonsensical jokes. His strong Boston accent (my birthplace) just adds to it.

Here are just a few of my favorite lines from this funny guy. You can find a huge collection on the web at Steven Wright Quotes.

And here are a couple of YouTube's I think you'll love.

Comic Relief Steven Wright Stand Up

Steven Wright – Just or Laughs

Appendix 5 - Silly Things to Do

(From my book, *Get Out of Your Thinking Box; 365 Ways to Brighten Your Life and Enhance Your Creativity*)

- Call a random number and just wish someone a nice day.
- Look at the world as if your eyes were on your knee caps.
- Have a "whine and Jeez" party.
- Come up with a nonsense language and use it with your friends.
- Listen to some old time radio shows (dumb.com).
- Go to a bank and ask for change for a nickel.
- Think of all the ways your life is like a *slinky*.
- Go skip rocks on a pond.
- Go test drive an 18 wheeler.
- Wear a silly hat all day.
- Spell check all your friends names and see what comes up. One of my friends' names came up as "cheery hormones".
- Interview some people telling them you are writing a book on some strange topic.
- Carry out a conversation with someone as if you are an opera singer.
- Pretend you are a sponge for a day and soak up everything you can. Wring yourself out at the end of the day. If your name is 'Bob" skip this one.

- Tap dance.
- Write down all the things that are bothering you on a roll of toilet paper – and flush it.
- Try your best to be dyslexic for a day.
- Think of some things that you've never thought about before.
- Build a model (plane, car, rocket etc.).
- Visit a cemetery and read the epitaphs.
- Create your own personal logo.
- Try to have a serious conversation with your dog or cat.
- Build a house of cards.
- Think of as many stupid questions as you can (even though there is no such thing as a stupid question).
- Browse through a library.
- Read a Dr. Seuss book.
- View the world from the perspective of an insect.
- Read a book of quotations. Start with my book, *Quotations to Tickle Your Brain*.
- Spend 15 minutes belly laughing for no reason at all.
- Pick a few objects around you and try to see what it would be like to be those objects.

Appendix 6 - Humorous Websites to Visit

Dumb.com – Endless fun with jokes, riddles, insults, and lots more

eBaums World - Funny videos, fail videos, funny pictures, funny galleries, funny links, flash **games**, jokes, caption contests, photoshop contests and much more.

Funny mail.com – Jokes of all types.

Bib Geek Daddy – A wonderful site for videos, many of them very funny.

GoComics.com – Your site for the best comics strips.

Cheesburger.com – Some pretty funny stuff!

Gocomics.com – Need some "comic relief". Go here for a while. Comics are updated every day.

Laugh Factory - A good selection of jokes of all kinds.

Funny Jokes and Quotes - Another great selection.

Jokeswarehouse,com - Need i say more?

That's a good start but there are lots more!

Appendix 7 – Funniest Movies Ever

Ace Ventura – Pet Detective

Airplane

Animal House

Big

Beverly Hills Cop

Blazing Saddles

Caddy Shack

Christmas Vacation

Fish Called Wanda

Happy Gilmore

The Jerk

Meet the Folkers

Monty Python and the Search for the Holy Grail

My Cousin Vinny

Naked Gun Series

Office Space

Pink Panther

Police Academy

Robin Hood - Men in Tights

There's Something About Mary

Space Balls

Sripes

Tommy Boy

Wayne's World

Young Frankenstein

Appendix 8 - Books on Humor

Anatomy of An Illness, Norman Cousins

Gesundhei!, Patch Adams

The Healing Power of Humor, Alan Kline

Laughter Therapy:; How to Laugh About Everything in Your Life That Isn't Really Funny, Annette Goodheart

Lighten Up; Survival Skills for People Under Pressure, CW Metcalf

Sniglets, Rich Hall and Friends, Collier Books, 1984

Stay Fit and Healthy Until You're Dead, Dave Barry

Note: Buy as many of Dave Barry's books as you can.

Totally Useless Office Skills. Rick Davis, Hobblebush Books, 1996

Appendix 9– Design of Humor Rooms

The majority of work areas are designed to be either very functional, or to look good. Creative thought doesn't tend to flourish in the typical sterile environment that fits these characteristics. Often people just need a place to escape to that allows them to just get outside of their normal thinking box. A number of organizations that I know of have created various designs for creativity or humor rooms. Kodak, John Deere, Ford, Hoechst Celanese are examples. I was the main driver behind the development of the Kodak Humor and Creativity Room in 1991. Let me share with you some of our thinking, and a bit about its development.

Why a humor and creativity room?

- It provides a place for people to go to think differently, and to find creative connections.
- It's a place for people to develop ideas, and to enhance their creativity and humor to enable them to be more effective in their work.
- It's a place for reducing the stress of everyday work.
- It provides an opportunity for networking and sharing ideas, and making connections between different thought communities.
- People are given the opportunity to lighten up, smile, and go back to their jobs with new perspectives.

- It creates an ideal and inexpensive area for group ideation sessions.
- It's a symbol that the organization is willing to extend its thinking into new areas. A sign that they are ready to explore possibilities, and create breakthrough.

In short, it's a place to get charged, recharged, excited, stimulated, humored, challenged, unstressed, turned on, and transformed. The important thing is to maintain a consistent connection between the work of the organization and the activities of the room. The room should exist for the purpose of building the creative capability of associates, and its eventual enhancement of the work they do.

The room needs to be a totally different environment from the normal. The original design of our Kodak Humor Room called for entrance through a hall of mirrors. Our thought was that this would change you to a different person as you entered. Although our budget didn't allow us to do this, everything we did do was an effort to make it different. We took out the false ceilings and overhead lighting that was in just about every other office location, and this alone made a dramatic difference. Bill Cosby, the Three Stooges, and a lot of pretty strange posters replaced pictures of George Eastman (the founder of Kodak). Furniture was an eclectic mix of second hand couches, chairs, and various art deco we collected from various sources. And we went out of our way to stay away from the typical neat office layouts. Although the room wasn't clearly sectionalized, there were four major themes.

The library area had a fairly large selection of books, and tapes, and some comfortable couches to sit in while browsing. There was no staff in the room. People were asked to not take things from the room and, on their honor, to return them if they did. Paper and chart pads were there for people to make notes, and our plans were to have a small copier available as well. Books included many useful publications on creative thinking along with a large selection of cartoons such as the *Farside* series. I would guess there were about two hundred books all together.

The presentation area had some comfortable seats for a couple dozen people, and the audio and video capability so we could play music, laugh tracks, comic routines, or various videos. Videos included Monty Python, Candid Camera, old time movies, and some serious creativity ones. We had a schedule of events published each week. There were also presentations from time to time on topics of interest regarding creativity and humor. The room was frequently used by groups engaging in ideation sessions, and it created a great environment for this.

We had the high tech section with a couple of PC's which were loaded with creativity and humor processing software. This wasn't as successful as I had anticipated, in part because people didn't have time to learn how to use the software. The intention was to eventually have some training sessions for those who were interested, but that never quite got off the ground.

And the fourth area was what we called our toy store. This included a substantial collection of items - some were in a particular section of the room and some scattered about the room. Items such as:

- spare body parts
- toys
- games
- hats (for viewpoint shifting)
- stress dolls
- punching bags
- silly items (such as laughing bags)
- mind teasers
- catalogues (for idea stimulating)
- animals and other objects
- objects for juggling (balls, scarves, hamburgers, chain saws etc.)

We located a number of easels around the room, and suggested certain ideas for these such as quotations, creative ideas for work, jokes, stories, and other things for people to share. We also had some that were there for group problem solving. Someone would write down a problem or opportunity, and people would write down ideas they had. The thing that perhaps stood out the most in the room was the old commode that someone found and dragged in. Apparently they felt that some of their best thinking took place there. So we put it in a corner of the room right under our collection of hats. When the NBC Today program highlighted the room, they showed one of our maintenance associates sitting on the thinking commode wearing a raccoon skin hat. I was skating on some pretty thin ice with some of the execs after that one.

Appendix 10

Comical Bumper Stickers

Ah, the world of bumper stickers. They have always fascinated me. Bumper stickers are a way of making statements and putting them out for the whole world around you to see. Here are a few of my favorites:

- Lottery: A tax on people who are bad at math.
- Consciousness: The annoying time between naps.
- Why is "abbreviation" such a long word?
- Be nice to your kids. They'll be choosing your nursing home.
- We all live downwind.
- If the people lead then eventually the leaders will follow.
- It's lonely at the top, but you eat better.
- Sometimes I wake up Grumpy. Sometimes I let her/him sleep.
- Change is inevitable, except in vending machines.
- Your kid may be an honor student but you're still an idiot.
- Why be normal?
- Subvert the dominant paradigm.
- Minds are like parachutes, they only function when open.
- My karma ran over your dogma.
- Everything I know is a result of my ignorance.
- Compost happens.
- Guns cause crimes like flies cause garbage.
- Rugby – elegant violence.

- They are not hot flashes – they are power surges.
- Enjoy life- this is not a dress rehearsal.
- A bad day fishing is still better than a good day at work.
- Alcohol and calculus don't mix. Never drink and derive.
- In dog years, I'm dead.
- Gravity – It's not just a good idea. It's the law.
- If at first you don't succeed, skydiving isn't for you.
- Get a new car for your spouse. It'll be a great trade.
- Old age comes at a bad time.
- The more you complain the longer God makes you live.
- Earth first! We'll strip-mine the other planets later.
- If you can read this I can hit my brakes and sue you.
- Sure you can trust the government. Just ask an Indian.
- If we are what we eat, I'm cheap, fast, and easy.
- Stop repeat offenders. Don't re-elect them.
- Fake it until you make it.
- Minds are like parachutes. They only function when open.
- Just undo it.
- We have enough youth. How about a fountain of smart?
- Question authority.
- Politicians and diapers need to be changed often for the same reason.
- Enjoy life. This is not a dress rehearsal.

- Forget world peace. Visualize using your turn signal.
- Stupidity should be painful.
- New York – where politicians make our license plates.
- If it wasn't for golf balls. how would we measure hail?
- What was the best thing before sliced bread?
- Ever stop to think, and forget to start again?
- Visualize whirled peas.
- Just think: In two days tomorrow will be yesterday.

I would be honored to have you review my book on Amazon.com. Reviews are very helpful, especially to fairly new authors like myself. My thanks to you in advance.

And check out my other books in this series, "Living Your Life To the Fullest", on my Amazon.com author page.

Other books in my *Living Your Life to the Fullest* series include:

A Little About the Author
Lindsay Collier

Lindsay was born and brought up in the Boston area. After graduating from Northeastern University with a BS in Mechanical Engineering he served as a Captain in the US Army Corps of Engineers. Following that he went to work for Eastman Kodak Company in Rochester, NY which he called home for most of his life. He was Kodak's *Technology Leader for Creativity, Innovation, and Strategic Exploration* and trained hundreds in creative thinking processes, and led many ideation sessions to help unleash the creativity of Kodakers. His interest in the connection between humor and work resulted in the development of the first corporate humor room. He took an early retirement after 25 years to begin a career as a writer and speaker.

Lindsay's first book, *The Whack-A-Mole Theory* was quite popular and also was translated to Japanese. He has been featured as a keynote speaker for dozens of corporations and organizations on the topic of creativity, innovation, and humor in the workplace. He also published a book called *Get Out of Your Thinking Box; 365 Things You Can Do to Brighten Your Life and Enhance Your Creativity* during this period.

After losing his first wife of 40 years, Jan, to ovarian cancer in 2000, he put his writing skills to work on his book, *Surviving the Loss of Your Loved One; Jan's Rainbow*. This book, along with his presentations on the topic, has helped hundreds of people deal with loss in their lives.

In 2005 Lindsay and his second wife, Jean, moved to The Villages, Florida. In 2014 he really caught the "writing bug". He published a book on organizational creativity, innovation, and change called *Organizational Mental Floss; How to Squeeze Your Organization's Thinking Juices. That was followed by Quotations to Tickle Your Brain*, a book where he shares some great quotes focusing on creative thinking, and *Organizational Braindroppings; Musings on Breakthrough and Change*.

In late 2014 he wrote *How to Live Happily Ever After; 12 Things You Can Do to Live Forever*, which he has turned into a presentation and workshop that has had rave reviews. He recent book, *Living Your Retirement Dreams and Growing Young in the Villages; Florida's Friendliest and Healthiest Hometown*, paints a great picture of this wonderful retirement community for those who are contemplated retirement - or for those who already live there. His new book, *Add Humor to Your Life; Add Life to Your Humor*, promises to be a landmark book on the power of humor in your life.

Lindsay's Amazon.com author page can be seen at **amazon.com/author/lindsaycollier**

And he can be reached at **lindsaycollier@comcast.net**

Made in the USA
Columbia, SC
02 February 2021

31181268R00085